THE COLLECTED POEMS OF
CATHY SMITH BOWERS

*For Mary – Here's to the
language that saves us –
Until our paths
cross
again –*

The Collected Poems of

Cathy Smith Bowers

Cathy Kanuga Feb 2014

The Love That Ended Yesterday in Texas
Traveling in Time of Danger
A Book of Minutes
The Candle I Hold Up to See You

Press 53

Winston-Salem

Press 53, LLC
PO Box 30314
Winston-Salem, NC 27130

First Edition

A TOM LOMBARDO POETRY SELECTION

Cover design by Kevin Morgan Watson

Cover art, "Cathy's Sunrise," Copyright © 2013 by Chuck Davis,
used by permission of the artist.

Author photo by Chris Bartol

"'The Sweet, Dark Center': The Poetry of Cathy Smith Bowers"
by Fred Chappell, first appeared in *Appalachian Journal,* Vol. 38.2-3
(Winter/Spring 2011). Used with permission.

Printed on acid-free paper
ISBN 978-1-935708-94-0

Contents

TRAVELING IN TIME OF DANGER

A Book of Minutes

THE CANDLE I HOLD UP TO SEE YOU

Acknowledgments

These poems first appeared in the following publications:

The Love That Ended Yesterday in Texas

The Davidson Miscellany, "The Girl Who Drove the Nail"
The Devil's Millhopper, "Birthright" and "Setting Things Straight"
The Georgia Review, "Aphasia," "Fall," "The Fat Lady Travels," "Hanging the Screens," "The Love," "Namesake," and "October"
Hiram Poetry Review, "Stars"
Iris, "Falling in Love with Sickness"
The Journal, "Mating Season on Firehorn Pond"
The Kenyon Review, "Men"
Pembroke Magazine, "To My Nephew, Age 11, of His Estranged Father"
South Carolina Review, "Markings"
Southern Humanities Review, "Turning the Myth Around"
Southern Poetry Review, "After Reading It Is Only a Myth That a Person Looking Up from the Bottom of a Well in the Middle of the Day Can See Stars," "Bone," "Elegy for My Brother," "One Hundred and Ten Degrees," "Paleolithic," "Third Child," "Saviours," and "Wanting Them Back"
The Wilmington Review, "The Flower We Could Not Name"
Poet Lore, "Thunder" and "To a Friend with a Hyphenated Last Name, after Her Divorce"
New England Review/Breadloaf Quarterly, "The Compass" and "Third Floor West"

Traveling in Time of Danger

Alkali Flats, "Kwanzaa," "Touring the Berliner Dom," "In Salzburg, Austria, a Student Learns His Father Is Dead"
America, "Mother Land"
The Atlantic Monthly, "The Entry" and "Learning How to Pray"
Emrys Journal, "Weather"
The Georgia Review, "You Can't Drive the Same Truck Twice," "Snow," and "Orchids"
The Greensboro Review, "Kingdom"
The New England Review, "For the Body"
Poet Lore, "Sequoia," "Pacific Time," and "Sleeping With My Brother"
Poetry, "A Southern Rhetoric"
Poetry Miscellany, "Them" and "Traveling in Time of Danger"
Shenandoah, "Easter"

The Southern Review, "Sponges," "Groceries," "Slow," "Peripheral Resurrections," "From Rome," and "The Scar"

Southern Poetry Review, "Women Dancing With Babies On Their Hips" and "Bark"

Third Coast, "Flood," "The Proposal," and "Three"

A Book of Minutes

The Atlantic Monthly, "Crepe Myrtles," "Mystery of the Sphinx," "Rosemary," "Yarrow," "Chamomile," "Horehound," "Sorrel," and "For My Dog Who Listens to All My Poems"

Main St. Rag, " 'By the Time We Get to Athens I'm Going to Look Like a Greek God,' He Said," "At a Topless Beach on Mykonos I Make a Deal With Jerry," "Driving Through the Mountains I Remember How My Friend Was Brought to Tears," and "Anatomy of a Southern Kiss"

Shenandoah, "The Eye," "The Skin," "Joint and Bone," "The Kidneys," and "Harvest Time"

The Southern Review, "When My Mother Speaks of Loneliness," "The Trunk," "Labor Day," "Flying to Sausalito With My Sisters," "Pansy," "Evening Primrose," and "Watching Bill's New Lover Prepare Our Evening Meal"

Southern Poetry Review, "I Ask Forgiveness of My Feet," and "For Okra"

Tar River, "How I Became an Existentialist," and " 'Give Uncle Wardy a Big Kiss,' Mama Said"

The Candle I Hold Up to See You

Asheville Poetry Review, "A Suit Our Brother Could Have Worn"

The Georgia Review, "The Napkin," "An American Family," "The Sabbatical"

English Journal, "Syntax," "Found Poem"

The Gettysburg Review, "Questions for Pluto," "Last Day," "The Notes," "How It Is in Their Clothes," "Pear Moonshine"

Nimrod, "Whistle-Speak"

Rapid River, "Solace," "Where's My Frog?" "All Adverbs, Adjectives Too"

Southern Poetry Anthology, "Shadow Dancing," "The Living Daylights," "First-Year Teacher"

Southern Poetry Review, "Cool Radio"

The Southern Review, "Abattoir," "Unmentionables," "Language: A Sentimental Education"

Wind, "My Brother's Star"

"The Sweet, Dark Center":
The Poetry of Cathy Smith Bowers
By Fred Chappell
North Carolina Poet Laureate (1997-2002)

Most critics and reviewers of poetry probably ought to be hanged, starting with me. When the early critical views of an interesting poet are collected at a later date, they are usually revealed as a bilge-soaked cargo of silliness, obtuseness, mistaken judgments, unlearned opinion, and stubborn incoherence. Yet where poets drift, critics are bound to sail after, reading the figures of their wakes in hopes to discern something of the sea-battered vessels that laid them. The problem is not always that the commentator is purblind; the exigencies of the duty are burdensome. Space is limited and so is time, if the remarks are to be published in journals. When the book under discussion is a first book, there is no body of work to furnish reference points, and it is difficult to form sound conclusions about a poet when only 50 or so examples of work are available.

For these reasons and for others less pardonable, I returned with dread to a few pages I had devoted to Cathy Smith Bowers' *The Love that Ended Yesterday in Texas* when it first appeared in 1992 from Texas Tech University Press. When it was reissued by Iris Press in 1997, some of my phrases were used as blurbage: "Her diction is ever the plainest, simple and sauceless ... She has foresworn rhinestone and sequins, but her lines are more comely for her modesty—and more moving too." This quotation is a fairly accurate summation of what I wrote, but it sounds like faint praise indeed—and the noun "modesty" is accurate only in the matter of Bowers' word choices. She was and is no shrinking violet.

Yet I was not completely wrongheaded. My list of some of her topics—"illness, death, dire trauma, catastrophe, old age, and disfigurement"—is sound enough, as far as it goes, but it hardly exhausts her mournful subjects, and it skates over them too glibly. All in all, I misread her book, emphasizing darkness as if she might have chosen it for its own sake. Bowers is not merely dark; most contemporary poetry is dark in tone. She is serious, as so many poets truly are not. Darkness chose her.

1.

A North Carolina Arts Council website sports a laconic biographical note and a glamorous photo of the state's new Poet Laureate. She succeeds the brilliant Kathryn Stripling Byer in that capacity and brings a different but still deeply genuine sensibility to it. We learn from the web posting that she was born in Lancaster, South Carolina, in 1949, one of six children of a textile-mill worker's family. She gathered the requisite academic degrees, began teaching high school, then moved to Queens College in Charlotte and joined the Creative Writing faculty there.

She has garnered a number of dignified awards and has published four collections. Those following her first are *Traveling in Time of Danger* (1999), *A Book of Minutes* (2004), and *The Candle I Hold Up to See You* (2009), all from Iris Press in Oak Ridge, Tennessee. She will cause comment and ignite spirits wherever she and her work appear. Cathy Smith Bowers is a tonic presence in Tar Heel and American poetry, and she is a comely representative for it.

It is handy to have this capsule biography, though most of the details could be gathered by reading her poems. Reading them might also inform us that she has traveled about the world as teacher and tourist and that she is a solid and enthusiastic teacher. The site mentions her "powerful poems about family and loss," naming her most frequent and often most disturbing subjects.

One of these is her mill-worker father and some hint of her thought about him may be gathered from the dedication to her first volume: "...for my mother / and / in odd, loving memory of my father." Those careful adjectives, *odd, loving*, allude to the fact that he was an alcoholic who seems, on the evidence of her pages, to have suffered severe depression. In "My Father's Last Wish," the speaker wishes she could hold the dying man "hostage" to his life-support mechanisms, "the way you held us all those years, / prisoners of your bitterness and rage" (*Traveling in Time of Danger* 97). *A Book of Minutes* presents a distressing snapshot of him at the kitchen sink, "shirtless and hung / over, his lungs // long gone to brown from double shifts." He asks his daughter to wash his back. She flees the task and that memory never deserts her. "Nights, still, I / lie in fear there / really is a // hell" (180).

A more frightening incident is recounted in "Fire" (*Texas* 55). The mother, busy in the kitchen making bread, smelled smoke and feared the worst. She ran to the children's bedroom and found the father in the closet, beating out with bare hands a fire he had set.

> For the insurance money, he told her later
> when she asked why he had done it.
> He wouldn't have let it hurt us, he said,
> or the rest of the house,
> just a few old clothes we could no longer wear. (*Texas* 55)

The mother is, of course, infuriated and would like to attack the drunken man physically, but she had lived through this kind of scene many times before, so

> all she did was take him to her breast
> and hold him, shaking her head,
> saying Edward, Edward. (*Texas* 55)

Bowers' gift for powerful understatement serves her well here, as elsewhere. Instead of pressing the moment to melodrama, she inserts phrases that distance us from the incident: "he told her later," "he said." When the poem ends with his name spoken twice by his wife, the focus of the whole shifts completely. "Fire" is no longer about the father's destructive behavior but about the mother's protectiveness and her nearly exhausted reserve of forgiveness.

The poet too is determined to forgive him, to the fullest extent that she is able. A poem in *Candle* recounts a dream in which she and her father accost St. Peter at the Pearly Gates after waking the venerable Guardian from a nap. When the saint demands to know "one good thing" the father ever did in his lifetime, the speaker searches her memory. Finally, she recalls an incident Bowers has also recorded in another poem: "the mutilated dog / he once shot to put it out of its misery" (261). Father and daughter stand waiting—and then the significance of the poem's title is revealed: "St. Peter Said, 'That's Good Enough,' and He Walked Through." Bowers' light hand is a blessing here. A poem expressing a hungry need to forgive could become mawkish with just a clumsy placement of commas, but this powerful wish-poem avoids sogginess with a sly pinch of wit.

The mother in these poems presents a sharp contrast to the figure of the father, though of course there are ambivalences in her treatments too. "Mother Land" is one of the warmest celebrations, the portrait of a large comfortable, comforting woman, "a continent, *terra softa* / where she sprawled in her big chair / or across the bed when thunder ripped / the shingles and rain swelled the sills" (*Traveling* 92). She is not only a comfort but a big, pillowy defense against the wild, pugnacious world of men.

> My mama
> was promised land and we, small redoubts
> not even our father could penetrate, odd denizen
>
> from that country of men we could see
> mounting the horizon, their bright
> flags flying, their cannons aimed. (*Traveling* 92)

The image of the mother as protector and comforter is almost a constant in Bowers' pages. One of the most striking examples is "Appropriate Container" (*Minutes* 227). The appropriate container her mother has requested from the speaker is to be used to hold the ashes of the poet's brother. Three years elapse before the poet finally chooses one, "swaddled // in the green velvet bag a friend / had once given / me wine in." The term *swaddled* is beautifully apt. The speaker presents the container, shrouded in spring flowers, and the mother accepts it, "Safe in / the soft crook of / her folded arm." This image is at once of a Madonna and Child and of a Pieta.

In "My Mother's Lexicon," we see the father through the mother's eyes—or, rather, through her language usage. It is an acutely telling poem, giving us a picture—somewhat distorted, perhaps—of the father's habitual behavior and the mother's attitudes toward it. We can gather something of the woman's background, her education and her rural heritage. The lines also show what delight our poet takes in vernacular speech, with its homely, sharply pointed phrases.

> You were the first poet, Mama.
> The language of

others never vociferous
enough. Dad didn't *patronize*
old man Causey's
bar, he *stayed laid*
up down there. Paid

not with cash but *rags from his younguns'*
backs. Not once did
he *come home,*
he *straggled in.* (*Minutes* 179)

Bowers recalls a colorful, salty idiom, and she invites the reader to join in her admiration. At the same time, though, she makes it clear her upbringing is a part of her background that does not control her own vocabulary, her present way of thinking. "Vociferous": that word was never the mother's.

This poem seems perfect in its dramatic compression, its steely economy, and in its cool yet sympathetic finesse.

Our roles in our families are likely to change as the years pass. The mother who has taught the child a pungent tongue must be taught by her daughter in the different circumstances that the title, "Aphasia," indicates. The mother must relearn even the most common words. "My mother whispers *clock, clock* / and points to the old refrigerator" (*Texas* 15). She loses ground continually: "Every day she drifts farther away, / the disease bearing her backwards." Yet the daughter will not give up. Persistence is one of her principal virtues and a prevalent theme in Bowers' poetry. She keeps trying, even though she probably knows her efforts must be in vain.

I give my mother my daughter's blocks.
Teach her square and round,
the simple symmetries of childhood.
Then candle, scissors, watch.
But for her, each is a flower
that closes in the night. (*Texas* 15)

Her mother, we must surmise, would consider, if she were able, that this painstaking re-education is no more than her due. When, in "A Southern Rhetoric," her daughter teases her about her countrified phraseology, she "shakes her finger" at the girl and *scolds her good.* "Girl, don't you forget who it was / learned you to talk" (*Traveling* 99). Then the mother turns away, "embarrassed," and the two of them remember, in different ways, that earliest time of learning:

> From the little house, the crib
> where she bent each day, naming
> for me the world where words always fail,
> warranting, now and then,
> those few extra syllables,
> some things spoken twice. (*Traveling* 99)

In these lines, the poet shows a little of the regret she feels about having teased her mother, and she now concedes that there are reasons to talk in the old-fashioned, naive way—and that there is a particular kind of beauty in the sentence her mother spoke: "It's a sight in this world / the things in this world / there are to see."

"Unmentionables" also takes as subject a singular habit of her mother's speech, her insistence upon euphemism. With words like "unthinkable," "unspeakable," and "unheard of" the mother attempts "to unsay the world" that her normal life witnesses and endures, the "pieces of unpalatable news / that daily [come] her way" (*Candle* 279). The word *leg* being "far too erotic / for her lexicon," she must refer to the foodstuff on the table as "*drumstick, dark meat, trotter.*" A neighbor woman is forced by poverty into prostitution and becomes the "*unfortunate down the street.*" When, late in life, the mother falls grievously ill, doctors plan to "amputate her lower / extremities," The daughter finds a cold and bitter comfort in the fact that mortality intervened and spared her "the indelicacy of those words, / mortification of a different kind." She never had to lose her *legs. Mortify* might well be a word the mother would use, but her background and personality would prevent her awareness of the pun.

Elegies and memorial poems are plentiful in Bowers' work. Besides those for her mother and father, her husband, and a friend named Beth Couvillion, more than a dozen concern the loss of her brother to an immune deficiency disease. The poet has a special regard for him, almost more than sisterly, perhaps because he was gay and thus set apart from the societal majority, just as poets are sometimes set apart. She seems to admire him too as an engaging and courageous personality. Some of her most moving poems are about her brother, but some of the strongest—"Kingdom," "Sleeping with My Brother," "My Brother's Star"—are too long to include here. Maybe one of the short ones in *Minutes*, "Labor Day," will give some sense of his lively appreciation of lovely things and of his courage in the face of death:

> Morning's IV done, all his pills,
> he turns to Bill's
> gift of Melon—
> icy sweet chunks
>
> of honeydew brought home from the
> local deli.
> I watch each bite
> he takes then wipe
>
> his chin. *Unbelievable*, he
> says and lifts a
> bite to me. Says,
> *here, just taste this.* (212)

2.

In "The Bill," the poet receives an itemized invoice from the funeral home that handles her father's remains. The amount comes to about $300, and she resents receiving such a demand since she felt so much like a stranger to the man. But she renders unto Pluto anyway, "knowing how sometimes / we're asked to pay up twice": "Once for what we never had. / Once for when it's taken back" (*Traveling* 98). She never really had a father, and consequently, she never really had a childhood in the way that children in more fortunate families supposedly do.

Bowers' poems mark many losses and one of the saddest of these is the missing childhood. It must be a strange, dislocating, and bitter feeling to mourn the loss of something you never had. "Wanting Them Back" compares the situation to being irritated by the continual "impenitent whine" of cicadas in late summer, but then in winter wishing to have them back again—"Like childhoods we wept to grow out of" (*Texas* 8).

In "Falling in Love with Sickness," she recalls the pleasures of convalescing when she was a child. She longed to contract "Flu and scarlet fever. / Diphtheria and mumps," as well as chickenpox, diabetes, malaria—diseases that would call her mother to her bedside, "bearing bowls of grapes and oranges, / that warm jar of mentholatum" (*Texas* 28). When these fond ministrations succeed in their purposes, the result is a hollow disappointment, almost a bereavement.

> I dragged myself from bed and slowly dressed, pausing
> to breathe the last sweet smells
> of the sickroom, then turning
> stepped quietly through health's lonely door. (*Texas* 29)

At one point the word "abattoir" became a talisman for her because as a child the enticing sound of it misled her about its meaning, suggesting "some faraway room / too lavish and exotic for the likes / of me" (*Candle* 251). It seemed related to "boudoir" and "armoire" and "reservoir," "places where things of value / might safely be kept. Chambers for dreaming / ladies. Wardrobes lush with dresses, hats, / and gowns." When the actual meaning of the term was revealed, she was "shocked / to learn there was also a place for misery / and pain." In the former time of innocence that is now destroyed, "Abattoir... / Abattoir... Abattoir" was a place so inviting she might have entered with eager anticipation, "stepped lightly in" (*Candle* 251).

As in "The Bill," she must lose what she never really possessed, something that never existed.

For me, her most poignant rendering of this theme is "Crepe Myrtles," in which a striking visual metaphor awakens an auditory memory that quickly fades away like an echo and takes a whole longed-for season of life with it.

> When the heaviness of dog days
> has had its way

with us, they bloom
to stay the doom

of summer's end. Such popsicles,
these crepe myrtles,
to cool the day's
parched tongue! And where's

the truck that brought them? The little
bell? Clang goes the
ghostly driver
and then is gone. (*Minutes* 225)

These spare lines present a homelier vision of longing and loss than A. E. Housman's "land of lost content," and I find Bowers' phrases more immediate and more moving than the classical scholar's abstractions.

In her volume-title poem, "Traveling in Time of Danger," she echoes, whether consciously or not, Housman's regretful plaint in similar geographical terms. The poem takes place in Budapest, where the speaker is overseeing a group of students on tour. The first Iraq war, Desert Storm, breaks out while they are there, and one of the students is panic-stricken. The poet assures her that there is little danger; in war time security is increased, "the safest / time to travel is in time of danger" (*Traveling* 145). The student cannot be placated; she is determined to rush back to America; she has already

called a cab
to take her to the airport where she'll wait,
counting her breaths, trusting the troops
already gathering, flooding
the gates and runways. Like the rivers
of that country she'll go home to,
the rivers that must have run there
in the first days of its life,
the first good days of its life. (*Traveling* 145)

The country the student will return to is not the same one she departed; war changes the character of countries and of people, including the young. The purity and confidence for which the formerly pristine rivers stand as emblem are now changed, their shining dimmed if not darkened.

Another version of her plangent theme, the loss of what was never possessed, finds one of its most poignant utterances in "Losses." The poem begins with a longish description of the poet's dog releasing its bowels first thing in the morning. The dog's posture in the act reminds the speaker of an incident in Indonesia where a woman "bathing / beneath the early rise Gunang Agung, / turned shyly away as our cameras continued to click" (*Texas* 45). She had accompanied her small child to the bank of the river "where he stooped like a little frog, emptying / his bowels onto the sand." Inexplicably, this sight gives rise to a premonition:

> Was it then I knew
> I would never have children? Could not bear
> at so close a range those leaks
> and solvents. Would get instead a dog
> I could train to go off into the woods
> carrying deep into shadow the body's chronic losses. (*Texas* 45)

The themes of childhood damaged or canceled, of the losses of what once was and what never was are frequent in Bowers' work. She has pondered them thoroughly, and her experience and meditation have given her insight into the situations and longings of others. The title of one of her treatments, "To My Nephew, Age 11, of His Estranged Father," outlines the situation, while the body of the poem enumerates the ways the young boy will mistake strangers for the father he no longer sees. The lad will imagine him as many figures: as a beggar on the street, as a bowman fighting two hundred warriors, as a pilot in a war film, a lineman among telephone wires, or "just the taxi driver / eating his peanuts / through the empty streets" (*Texas* 50).

The poem closes on an ominous note. His powerful longing may lead the nephew into such dangers as he has been warned about: "You know where / he would take you / and still / you want to go" (*Texas* 50).

An edgy variation on the theme of losing what was not possessed, of longing for what seemingly can never happen, occurs with "Bone." This poem bears as epigraph a sentence from a "Laundry List" for children of alcoholics: "We became addicted to chaos after living in the midst of trauma" (*Texas* 40). The opening lines describe the daily situation, as it was with the speaker's father:

> Our house was a needle's eye
> you shoved a camel through.
> You gave us each a bone.
> Arm finger toe and ankle
> to be tucked in childhood's baggage
> and lugged around from day to day. (*Texas* 40)

But after a longish time, the situation changed:

> When you finally died
> we were surprised
> at the benignancy of doors,
> passivity of pots and pans. (*Texas* 40)

A "normal," much-desired way of living made its way into the house, the blessing of peacefulness so fresh and strange as to be palpable. Bowers embodies the feeling in a startling and disturbing image: "The quiet you left / hunkered in corners / like sacks of tongueless kittens" (*Texas* 40). The fate of kittens put into sacks is well known, and the reference seems incongruous to a scenario in which peacefulness has been so long and ardently wished for. But how can we enjoy peace if we have never known it? How can we be certain that we understand what it is? Perhaps it is too ponderous a blessing for us to be able to accept.

> For a while we kept our distance,
> trying hard to love the silence
> then one by one
> we gathered with our sticks
> and began to poke. (*Texas* 40)

A childhood lost can never be reclaimed; reclamation requires memories and if they are poisonous, they will be avoided, when that is possible. Yet they must be faced sooner or later, and that confrontation will not be peaceful. How does one reconcile with a time now vanished, a time inimical to hope and joy? If it were possible to oppose it in present time with physical violence, such action might afford a measure of relief. A remote prospect that, but Bowers does find one situation in which the fantasy is played out.

It is clear that she sympathizes and, in large degree, identifies with the children in "The Party" (*Texas* 9). The poem tells of a social affair that a group of college students arranged "for some battered / children the department of social services rounded up." The children are intimidated by the strange surroundings and the clumsy Santa. "He kept ho-ho-ing, / urging the children into the fun, but they hung / at the edge of the room." The picture Bowers presents could be an image out of Dickens:

> Their hands
> and faces had been scrubbed, and still
> they looked soiled, their hair the color of titmice,
> the washed-out skin, shoulders dangling
> like wire hangers beneath their shirts and blouses. (*Texas* 9)

The party is a doleful failure, and none of the proposed games entice the children until the appearance of "the bright piñata, the crepe bull / spinning from the light." At this point, the children joined furiously in,

> went at it with their sticks, fevered,
> like a small tribe at the beginning of time
> flailing and beating until the soft hide broke
> spilling out onto the floor its sweet, dark center. (*Texas* 9)

"The Party" admits of an allegorical reading in which the downtrodden of the world can acquire some of their just desserts only through violent action. But though Bowers does venture into allegory now and again—as in, for instance, "Questions for Pluto" in *Candle* and "To the Oldest Live Oak in the South" and "Peace Lilies" in *Minutes*—she mostly stays away from such constructions, content to allow situations and dilemmas to embody their own narratives, and for observed details to suggest and bolster their own weighted meanings.

This latter practice is common among contemporary poets who distrust allegory and overt symbolism as being "literary" devices that violate a certain hazy standard of genuineness. While it is true that allegory is liable to become mechanical and nonsuggestive and that easy symbolism may lead to preachment, the standard contemporary practices have their drawbacks too. Often we find poems made from anecdotal material. In fact, the only thing that prevents them being mere anecdotes is that the poet leaves out information in the interest of economy and, perhaps, mystery. Sometimes what remains are puzzling accounts, with omitted material to be supplied by chat during public readings. Bowers rarely commits such irritating nuisances, though "The Entry" and "In Salzburg, Austria, a Student Learns His Father Is Dead" come close (*Traveling* 144, 146).

3.

My untidy essay here shuffles the poems into loose categories, poems about family, poems about a lost childhood. Such divisions are obviously artificial and often strained. The childhood theme will inevitably involve material about the family, and it composes a large part of another theme, the wish.

A great many lyrics can be read as wishes and prayers simply because imagination must show alternatives to present realities in order to make comparisons; the purpose of the suppositional comparison is to try to understand the present circumstances. The Garden of Eden is a picture of what our world might be, the myth of the Golden Age a picture of what our own age is lacking.

The poem "Aphasia" (*Texas* 15) I cited as a facet of the relationship with the mother, the child teaching the mother language by means of toy blocks. This touching poem includes an unfiltered wish, as Bowers recalls a botany class in which "old Professor Zaroff" would reverse his instructional film, "backwards / faster and faster." For the poet, this is an image of the mother's loss of her memory that closes up each night like a flower. Like the flower in the reversed film, the mother's past whirs backward using itself up, as

> dewy petals quivered, curling
> into the slender pistil, into

the whorled womb of calyx
retreating into leaf
into stem and bulb

until nothing was left
but a small mound of earth
and the sun and the moon
chasing each other
across the exhausted skies. (*Texas* 16)

For an individual, the loss of memory is the same as the end of time. For the daughter to watch her mother in the grip of forgetfulness is like watching the end of the world. Here, the usual wish to turn time backward is put aside because for the mother time does indeed run backward, and the result is disastrous. The sentimental couplet by Elizabeth Chase Allen—"Backward, turn backward, O Time in thy flight, / Make me a child again just for tonight"—is fulfilled in Bowers' poem, but not with happy result.

In "Setting Things Straight" (*Texas* 64), the mother's wish is simpler: "She wants the planets / all in place once more, / the moon and stars aligned."

One of the strongest of the wish-poems is "Third Child," in which the speaker wonders what it would be like to have another sibling. "It might have been a sister. / One who would have let you wear her clothes. / Crinolines. Pearl-studded collars" (*Texas* 66). The reverie continues and includes an episode in which the imaginary sister teaches the speaker about menstruation.

This third child might "have been the one to save" them all. Perhaps it would have been a second brother.

A good one this time.
Face too soft for battering.
Heart so sweet it would have gathered
the broken family in
the way street people, wintering,
migrate from under bridges,
from out of bags and boxes
to huddle about a flaming bin. (*Texas* 66)

The Candle I Hold Up to See You opens with a sequence of wish-poems called "Eight Names for God." The eight are names taken from the Kabbalah, and each fulfills a different function. The first allows us to go back in time; the third voices a hope that miracles really happen; the fifth name restores health; the seventh restores a broken world; and I wonder if the Jewish pious might not have called upon this latter name when the World Trade Towers fell, although the poem was written before that date.

> Yes, this is the name
> that will raise again the beams,
> conjure the girders' strength,
> render whole the shattered window
> panes, calling back into essence
> the bright fragmented brilliance
> of our lost selves. (*Candle* 243)

Bowers' wish-poems are not often so broad in their intentions; she is generally a poet of the personal, narrowly focused thrust of impulse. In "Weather," we see her narrowing her focus by stages. Beginning with an account of early civilized history ("the ancient Egyptians / knew God was nothing / more than weather") that includes also "the bug-eyed Sumerians," she moves to a broad historical perspective of barber shops which hum all day with "that old confession of weather" (*Traveling* 107).

Then she personalizes the concept. "It's no wonder the last love / of my grandmother's life / was the weatherman on the local channel." This friendly grandmother used to relay the television forecast to passersby "as she rocked on the porch." W. H. Auden once mentioned weather as the most interesting as well as the most boring of subjects for conversation, and Bowers celebrates it as a medium of neighborly exchange with her grandmother.

> And no wonder each would stop a moment
> out of their busy lives
> to listen, to smile and nod
> before moving on, taking with them
> that small gift of weather, that prayer. (*Traveling* 108)

No prayer is spoken here, of course, but implicit in the grandmother's report is a wish that all will be well with those she knows; her meteorological report is a prayer for their happiness.

The idea of the wish as prayer is presented more explicitly and more urgently in "Learning How to Pray." The poet had never been prayerful, had "even as a child / snubbed Mama's mealtime ritual." But when she receives news that her brother is dying, she begins to pray to every deity she has heard about, Buddha, Shiva, Vishnu, Isis, the "god of Ishmael," "the Druid reverence," even to *our carbon who art in heaven* (*Traveling* 119). Her wish that her brother live is so powerful it leads her into "promiscuity" of gods. If such acceptance of so many beliefs is sacrilegious, so be it. She still must pray for her brother.

> I could not stop
> myself   I like a nymphomaniac
> the dark promiscuity
> of my spirit   there
> for the taking   whore
> of my breaking heart   willing
> to lie down   with anything. (*Traveling* 119)

"Learning How to Pray" is one of her most wrenching pieces, perhaps the one in which the poet speaks most nakedly from her own person, obliterating as much of the distance as possible that a work of art inevitably sets between itself and its audience. It is so openly confessional that it amounts to something of an anomaly in Bowers' work.

When her wish-poems turn away from personal predicaments, they lose some of their intensity, though they still retain her warm and ready sympathies. "The Fat Lady Travels" (*Texas* 63) is a sketch of a character type. "On any train / she is the occupant / of either seat." In a later line, "She is all of Brodbingnag." Bowers is more interested, however, in the inner person in the exorbitant flesh. "When she dreams / she is never the goddess / turning men into pigs. / She is the pig."

The closure of "Fat Lady" is a wish built upon a fantasy conceit, that the woman might divide in two.

What she should lose
would be enough
to make the sister
she never had. (*Texas* 63)

This twinned figure would be a sibling loving and agreeable, like the fantasy sister in "Third Child," and, as in that poem, they would have fun together, once they were two.

And how thin
the both of them would be
gliding on fine-point skates
across some fragile pond

and, oh, it holding! (*Texas* 63)

The design of the poem makes it into a wish on the poet's part that this lady might find happiness, if only in her fantasies. It is much like the wish inherent in the weather report the grandmother passes on to her neighbors.

"I want a life that slow" is the wish spoken in "Slow" (*Traveling* 151). The slowness desired is the rate of speed referred to in a favorite joke about the turtle who, having been mugged by a snail, could not give a coherent account "*because it all happened so fast.*"

I want a life that slow. To lumber
each morning out of the slush
and mire, my earthly possessions
strapped across my spine. (*Traveling* 152)

It is an honorable wish, to want to be as simple as possible, and another is to be as truthful as an idiot savant named George who always swore to the facts he recited, "the wreck of his old hand rising toward the sky." The speaker vows to seek out her true friends, the ones who beg her to tell her snail-turtle joke again. "*Stop me if you've heard this,*" she will say, but they will not stop her, "happy / with this old joke, this weather, / this truth I've told, again" (*Traveling* 152).

A Book of Minutes provides a wish-poem that carries a caveat inside its prayer. It is addressed "To St. Brendan the Navigator, Protector of Sailors" (171). According to his legend, Brendan is the saint who brought Christianity across the perilous seas to Ireland. Some accounts make out that his vessel was a stone watering trough. As in others of Bowers' poems, there is a yearning for a better world. But the wish is not pure because it includes an acknowledgement of the imperfections carried by those in quest of paradise.

> Who among us has not tossed for
> years, bereft, your
> kind, adrift in
> the foamy brine,
>
> searching for some strange and perfect
> world where we might
> begin anew,
> unaware there
>
> is always a veil that hides the
> paradise we
> seek, that always
> we are the veil. (*Minutes* 171)

But this poet is a realist. She does not confuse even her most ardent wishes with the facts of the case, and she looks upon the wishes with a healthy measure of skepticism. However much she tries to enjoy them whole, she recognizes that she is trying to force a belief, as she did back in 1986, waiting for the appearance of Halley's comet (*Texas* 69): "And again I am a schoolgirl / trying hard to believe / what the eye cannot see."

4.

For most of us, the readiest trigger of wishes and fantasies is probably sexual desire. Cathy Smith Bowers is a nifty erotic poet, and her love poems add brio to volumes that, shadowed with regretful reminiscences, can be rather somber.

My first introduction to her erotic verse came during a public reading celebrating the 50th anniversary of *The Georgia Review.* I was seated next to an earnest young lady, perhaps a student on assignment, who had paid close attention to all the poets who trailed to the podium. She was taking copious notes. Naturally, I was curious about her reactions and surreptitiously read what she wrote down.

She listened intently as Bowers read "Fat Man in the Sauna," a poem that begins grayly: "How strange the aloneness / of that day" (*Traveling* 138). The lonely day is Christmas; the speaker has gathered "the final papers" of her divorce proceedings and "checked in / to the Renaissance Hotel, alone." She exercises in the hotel gymnasium and afterward goes to the sauna, where she finds the fattest man she had ever seen,

> beardless and bald,
> his white groin swaddled, half sitting,
> half reclining in the cedary-sweet
> warmth of the sauna, slowly eating
> an apple. *Come in* he said, calmly,
> quiet between bites, between
> the skin's delicate breaking
> and the soft ruminations
> of his tongue. *Come in* he said.
>
> And I went in (*Traveling* 138)

My young lady waited until the entire poem was read, then made a single notation: "SEXPOT." She underlined the word.

Her interpretation was a little naive, I think. To me, the theme of the poem is self-renewal, in this case, the necessity to seek out new experiences to supplant too-customary memories of an unhappy relationship. In short, I take it to be a poem about the thirst for knowledge, and my earnest young listener was distracted from pursuing this line of thought by the ostensible subject matter.

Not that Bowers would hesitate to write a lyric in which the theme was openly sexual—she is as straightforward in her treatment of love as in her presentations of other subjects. "Evening Primrose" is a playful example of her cheerful eroticism.

Statutory flower, I tease
my husband as
he leans in close
and softly blows

into a still half-open bud.
Be patient, would
you, I whisper
as she quivers

to full blossom beneath his breath.
He turns to me
and smiles. A warm
breeze lifts my dress. (*Minutes* 198)

Romantic love is a constant and important theme in Bowers' work. Her first book takes its title from a passage of Thomas Wolfe, and "The Love" develops the subject with a lengthy exercise in personification. "The love that ended yesterday in Texas / crawled out of the sea / fresh-eared and barnacled," it begins and then follows the journey of the strange sea-creature as it traverses glaciers and winds through mountains, through gorges and canyons, and survives a long geological history to end up "here," in a corner near the jukebox, "where he sits / mourning the woman / whose voice, like the sea, / still calls him" (*Texas* 22). It is only an elaborate, fanciful conceit on the fond notion of love that endures forever in its avatars, but "The Love" possesses a wry charm that is the hallmark of many of Bowers' pieces. She makes poems that are classy and funky at the same time.

With "The Scar," the approach is different. It begins with a description of a lover's body that the speaker finds beautiful and in one important detail very similar to Michelangelo's statue of David. "We were eighteen then," she says, and she had never seen anything so perfect as the body of her lover. The fact that the perfection carried a surgical scar only emphasized how *humanly* beautiful this form was. Pondering upon it, she comes to a realization, "the wisdom / of old philosophers, how what is real / exists only in the realm of the unchanging" (*Traveling* 127). But her man's humanity is a part of his Platonic ideal form, and the scar is a sign of that unity, "lifting and falling, / that lovely, immutable banner of his breathing."

Both "The Love" and "The Scar" refer offhandedly to the Renaissance doctrine of the ladder of love, the notion that earthly beauty, attracting us by pleasurable slow degrees, leads us to ascend to the ideal true beauty that lies behind appearance. This concept lit up the sensibilities of Dante, Petrarch, Sidney, and many another star-gazing bard, including most particularly W. B. Yeats.

Bowers does not stay perched on the highest rungs of the Platonic ladder. On one side of her nature, she is too earthly and too experienced in the ways of the world to place all her belief in Platonic idealism. She has a streak of Byron in her, and her hard-won self-knowledge comes to bear upon her love poetry.

"Ascension" is a bittersweet remaking of Apuleius's myth of Cupid and Psyche in which the true identity of the god of love, once revealed, ruins the relationship beyond repair. In Bowers' poem, the speaker has taken a very spiritual-seeming lover, all "moondrift and solar," "his frame an anorexic girl's."

> One night I awoke to find him
> in the flung doors of the balcony.
> He had taken the gauze curtains
>
> from their rods and draped them across
> his shoulders, his arms spread against
> the moon's soft rising like the wings
>
> of some angel or bat. (*Traveling* 134)

That alternative choice, "or bat," gives the tale away. When he is absent the next morning, she at first imagines he has ascended to a "place / of peace and light." But then she is rudely disillusioned, seeing "the four muddy ruts of his retreads," and realizes "he had taken the truck instead."

Even so, disillusion is not the principal theme of "Ascension." The tone is gently self-mocking, and the tenor of the whole makes it clear that the speaker regards the sport as well worth the risks. She also provides one bright picture of true and constant romantic love, a view of what must be a happy relationship that endures over a long period of time. The title, "Touring the Berliner Dom, January, 1990" sets the scene in which Bowers places her narrative. A group of tourists descends into a cathedral crypt to visit "the scattered bones / of emperors, bones of their Sons / and daughters" (*Traveling* 141). These were impressive sights, certainly, but what struck her most vividly was an incident that took place afterward at the perimeter of the tour group, when

> a man, aged seventy, knelt
> at his old wife's feet,
> slowly on one knee
> and tied her shoe, looped
> one string carefully
> across the other
> and pulled it through, tightening
> the worn laces into a solid bow. (*Traveling* 141)

This is one of the most artful placements of action in a lyric poem that I have ever come across. It owes much to film technique, of course. The brief vignette takes place in daylight after the tour group has climbed out of the darkness of the crypt. The gesture is described meticulously; the effect, after the purposefully jumbled action of the first 18 lines of the poem, is one of slow-motion photography in extreme close-up. The pose of the couple is the traditional pose of a man asking a woman's hand in marriage, and the knot that is tied, the "solid bow," stands as a renewal of their vows. Then the camera is moved for a medium-long shot that includes the group, and we see the conclusion of the action through the group's awareness:

> We stood there quiet and watched him
> tie her shoe, pat it, then turn gently
> to the still-tied other one and tighten it, too. (*Traveling* 141)

This is a poem that will cause the grouchy denizens of college creative writing classes to howl derisively. "Sentimental! Gutless! Untruthful! Schmaltzy!" Upon hearing such execrations, Bowers should swell with pride.

Let me see if I can mollify that callow arrogance of writing students with a poem a little sexier in tone, one that suggests but does not barge into the graphically literal, a verse that might have been inspired by Catullus, or that might, if the millennia could be reversed, inspire him.

In Praise of Bald Men

Glory be to God for shiny
things. Sweet orbs. Sweet
sublunary
spheres devoid of

mundane hair. Come, my brilliant one,
trust me now whose
hungry fingers
navigate what

luminates each night our astral
bed. Whose tongue must
needs explore such
heavenly head. (*Minutes* 196)

If my note-taking young friend had heard this poem read down in Athens, Georgia, I think she might have underlined SEXPOT! twice more and added a couple of excited exclamation points.

5.

Someone reading my pages here might wrongly conclude that I regard this poet as artless. I have emphasized the plainness of her diction, her usual avoidance of fancy formal constructions and elaborate metaphors, and her level-gaze presentations. She does not hanker after ornamentation and is not partial to qualifiers. In one poem, she agrees warmly with her step-daughter who, in a moment of pique, declares that she hates "All Adverbs, Adjectives Too" (*Candle* 269).

She has determined to obliterate all gestures, impulses, and feigned tendencies toward pretension. She vaunteth not herself, nor for that matter, does she write lines that aggrandize the importance of poetry. She is too utterly serious about the art to make pronouncements about it. Every now and then, as in "For My Dog, Who Listens to All My Poems," she will prick with a glistening pin even her modest claims.

> How entranced, each time, she sits there,
> her eyes, I swear,
> filling with tears
> at her master's
>
> inimitable brilliance. It's
> clear to me what's
> bounding through her
> head: *The greatest,*
>
> *yet, of all the generations!*
> My husband says
> she's just waiting
> for her rations. (*Minutes* 188)

Well, more than a few poets pretend to hide their lights under bushels. Sometimes, though, when you lift the bushel, you find only a dreadful darkness underneath. Sometimes a modesty of means betokens a modesty of import. But Cathy Smith Bowers uses a modesty of presentation and an economy of means in the interest of saying something genuine. Nor does she confuse sincerity with honesty. What she says, she means and knows that if she said more she might actually mean less.

"Pear Moonshine" is a poem I shall offer as touchstone. It is entirely characteristic, in presentation as well as in the power of its unmistakably genuine feeling. It is an elegy, a celebration of friendship, an offering of gratitude, and a beautiful demonstration of catharsis and the possibility of renewal. It takes place on a winter night when her husband is "not three cycles dead" (*Candle* 295). Two friends, Sue Campbell and Candy Butler, knock on her kitchen door and enter, "bearing gifts." One gift is homemade soup; the other is what the title designates, "a jar of swollen pears embalmed / in liquid fire" (295). The trio adjourns to "the living room by the hearth" to open the jar.

It is a dire shame upon me now to unsheathe my blackboard pointer instead of letting the poem speak all on its own, but I feel compelled to draw attention to a few tropes because for all their resonant implications, Bowers has, by careful assimilation, made them unobtrusive: "the gold corona," "The ghostly triad," "the waning jar," "the glacier of my pain."

> Sue
> led me to the living room by the hearth
> as Candy spun the gold corona
>
> of its lid, drank deep and passed
> the jar to Sue then on to me, the ghostly
> triad of our lips leaving their own
>
> soft crescents along the rim. Outside
> no star had yet to show, no other
> moon to light the snow that all day
>
> long had kept me weeping close
> to the sputtering flames. We drank
> and passed the waning jar and drank
>
> again until the glacier of my pain
> began to break, a thousand icy floes
> drifting down the river of my grief
>
> and then we ate the soup. (*Candle* 295)

Hardship, cruelty, heartbreak, bleak sorrow—these sad themes are plentiful in the pages of Cathy Smith Bowers. But in its smoldering heart, her poetry holds, like the piñata in "The Party," a "sweet, dark center."

THE LOVE THAT ENDED
YESTERDAY IN TEXAS

For Dennis
and
for my mother
and
in odd, loving memory of my father.

Subtract us into nakedness and night
again, and you shall see begin in Crete
four thousand years ago the love
that ended yesterday in Texas.

—Thomas Wolfe
Look Homeward Angel

~~~ REMEMBERING EARTH ~~~

PALEOLITHIC

We love these old caves—Lascaux,
Altamira—and walk carefully
the way we always enter the past,
our hands bearing
the artificial light of this world.

We imagine those first hunters
crouched, conjuring luck,
carving into rock-swell
their simple art—whole herds of bison,
the haunches, the powerful heads, floating
orderless along the walls.
And some are climbing sky
as if they were stars, planets
orbiting something they cannot see.
Centuries will pass before they
right themselves, their hooves
coming down onto the deep
wet floor of leaf-fall.
Remembering earth.
Remembering where it was
they were headed.

WANTING THEM BACK

In September we grew sick
of the cicada's impenitent whine,
the beetle's clicking,
raw thorax and bumble of harvestfly.

Even the hummingbirds
buzzing like neon thumbs
around the bulbs of sweetened water
we had hung from the gutter ledge.
Good riddance, we said
when they left for Mexico.

Now, as early as December
we are tired of talking to ourselves,
of the body's noisy machinations,
the blood knocking
like a tribe of pygmies beating sticks.

One morning we find ourselves at the window,
staring up at sky's vacant lot,
wanting them back.
Like childhoods we wept to grow out of.

Like the man who looked on
as the boy he had carved from pine
turned suddenly flesh,
his painted-on hair bristling to life
as he leapt to the floor running,
astonished at the ruckus in his chest,
at the strange old man at his back
who kept crying *Be wood! Be wood!*

THE PARTY

Perhaps it was that song those stars
recorded, their arms entwined like ivy,
swaying, their words a joyous proclamation
of brotherhood. Or something some professor
said in class about what it means to be a citizen
of this world. Anyway, for some reason
that was the year I became magnanimous.
The students were throwing a party for some battered
children the department of social services rounded up,
a small herd of defective cattle
we would prod into the season with gifts and song.
The beard the president of the club had strapped
clumsily on jutted from his chin like a shovel
of dirty snow. His red suit, stuffed with clothes
his fraternity no longer wore, preceded him
into the room like the belly of a man
who has given his life to food. He kept ho-ho-ing,
urging the children into the fun, but they hung
at the edge of the room, a neighborhood
they were afraid to step out of. Their hands
and faces had been scrubbed, and still
they looked soiled, their hair the color of titmice,
the washed-out skin, shoulders dangling
like wire hangers beneath their shirts and blouses.
Odd, how, like that bad joke about blacks
and orientals, they all seemed to look alike
huddled there against the wall, as if poverty and pain
like hunched backs were a matter of wrecked
genetics. Odder still, how, when the other games failed
and they were coaxed to the bright piñata, the crepe bull
spinning from the light, they joined furiously in,
went at it with their sticks, fevered,
like a small tribe at the beginning of time
flailing and beating until the soft hide broke
spilling out onto the floor its sweet, dark center.

STARS

There are darknesses here
no one has ever known
like the town
in that strange novel
when the world was so new
things did not yet have names.

Like the room
where my mother's mother
pieced quilts by candlelight
to document her passing.

Tonight, late August,
the month that leaves the skies unseamed,
we spread on a grassy hill
her eight-point star,
so perfect in its symmetry,
each star's bright center holding
as if to verify
such heavens could be tamed.

We expect meteors,
light in all defiance of design,
want stars arcing the sky so wide
our mouths will fill with dust.

You see a bear
and a man who holds
against his ever hopeful breast
that bright bear's death.

I see six sisters
and know the one that's lost
is lost forever.

We lean back into a place
so void of light
it has no name.

Above us sky hangs on its rack,
tattered, threadbare.
That old thing.

TIME

The first time I knew
it could not be trusted
I was sick on chocolate rabbits
and a basket of dirty eggs
I had fumbled all morning
on the cemetery's immaculate lawn—
some kind of service for watching the sun rise.

What's Easter? I asked my mother
then stood with my eyes agape
as the words rolled away from her mouth.
Having asked only months before
What's Christmas? it was years
before I could erase from my mind
the horrors I envisioned—a fat, pink
baby Jesus squiggling on a cross.

That fall, a great great aunt
appeared like impetigo out of nowhere
sweet and festering in the heat of dog days.
She moved slow as altar call.
She was old as a railroad tie
across whom the years had clanged and rattled.

As dusk fell and I tumbled in the dewing grass
she rocked on the porch with my mother
and remembered how she, too, deaf
to her mother's distant voice,
had made light of dark.

It was only yesterday I heard her cry
as my mother dragged me to bed.
All night I prayed against tomorrow,
against facing at the breakfast table
that rag of skin nailed to those old bones.

BIRTHRIGHT

As early as ten it started.
That fine blue line
on the back of my calf,
that line I thought
my mark of immortality.

Not your voluptuous breasts,
not the heart-shaped lips,
not the plump, soft hands
extended to the world:
Help, here is help for all your needy.

When I was twenty
they told me you were dying.
Half my blood would not
bring you back to life.

Tangle of blue vines.
Mesh of chicken wire.
Bloody wandering jew.
Fish net slung out to dry
on a ragged pier

till year by year
it spread
on the banks of my spindly calf.
A rivulet, a gorge,

bright glacier moving
down the plain of my smooth leg,

my personal cartographer
mapping out the highway of my life.

Mother, look.
Here below the awkward knee
lies the road to Avernus

where you wait
for this body, your proud vessel,
this blood, your Acheron.

APHASIA

My mother whispers *clock, clock*
and points to the old refrigerator
with its hisses and bumps and screeches
we mistook one night for a wild turkey,
fearing all of nature had moved inside.

Every day she drifts farther away,
the disease bearing her backwards
like those schools of salmon
she knew in her girlhood,
their lean and shadowy bodies
leaping the difficult falls.

One by one, names fall away from faces,
each a sloughed-off skin,
a small star burning out. I gather
her words like scattered toys,
jangle them before her eyes,
a ring of bright keys.

I give my mother my daughter's blocks.
Teach her *square* and *round,*
the simple symmetries of childhood.
Then *candle, scissors, watch.*
But for her, each is a flower
that closes in the night.

Like that film old Professor Zaroff
kept showing years ago in botany class—
roses, lilies, azaleas
unfolding before our eyes.
Then, his hysterical laughter
echoing through the corridors,

he began running it backwards
faster and faster, the screen
relinquishing everything
to the whirring reels.

I sat in the dark and watched
as dewy petals quivered, curling
into the slender pistil, into
the whorled womb of calyx
retreating into leaf
into stem and bulb

until nothing was left
but a small mound of earth
and the sun and the moon
chasing each other
across the exhausted skies.

ONE HUNDRED AND TEN DEGREES

Desert moved into town
and made itself at home.
Houses glowed like skulls.
Banisters lined the stoops
like rows of teeth.

Lizards died
and a mongrel dog nobody claimed
whose bones we offered up
like the bodies of virgins.

Our morning prayers
toppled off our tongues
like ancient dances.

Soon, we gave up old religions,
divided what little faith was left
between the sun
who rode her flaming broom
across the sky

and the train,
its empty boxcars
the dark, cool mouths of saviours
luring us inside.

OCTOBER

No rain for months.
We are dry as when our fathers
swore off booze.
As when our mothers permed our hair
and left us up too long.
We get nervous around matches.

In the shortened days
the trees grow pornographic,
think their time is up,
last chance for love.

They pull on wigs
as red as Orphan Annie's
before her eyeballs failed,
gather faded skirts about their throats,
flash us with what's been too long under—
silk petticoats and panties,
bright contraband imported
by the underworld.

This trick they turn is old.
We are seasoned to it
and do not shock.

The sun, to stave off boredom,
has taken another route,
pulls up in his sequined limousine
and stops.

The leaves
think they have somewhere to go
and start to fall.

TURNING THE MYTH AROUND

for Dr. George Archibald, who "courted" a whooping crane to get it to ovulate

I had hoped for a god
like Leda's.
Huge wings bearing down,
great beak against
the feathers of my throat
transforming me
into the swan
I had always dreamed.

But here's this clumsy mortal
who flails and beats
the air all day
into a thousand shards of light
he must be drowning in.

Still, when the sunlight
falls against his human face,
his eyes ablaze
in the heat of a ritual dance
he has come to love,

something shifts inside me,
begins to move,
like stars thrown out
against the night
where a species of dwindling gods
mourn their own endangered race.

THE BIRTHMARK

for my niece

At first we made stories about it.
How in heaven you sold flowers
at the harp maker's gate.
How this one
must have
fluttered
from your hand
clinging
to the moist
new earth of your skin
as you tunneled
my sister's body
into this life.
Year by year it grew
listing your tiny ankle
like a sorrel bloom.
Changed.
Became iris.
Became violet.
Black mutation of rose.
Soon, it resembled no flower
we could name.
Drifted.
Small island
up the pale wash of your shin,
its beauty darkening
like a song
no man, unbound,
would ever want to hear.

Alzheimer's

All day long
he watches from his window
the small red boat
he thinks is burning.

Its painted flames
flash bright as quills
making history of air.

Every day
the boat comes back
ablaze.

If only he
could get outside,
touch ground,
he's sure his feet
would anchor him to earth,
furrow deep as knotted roots,
the cambium of his heart
ringing another year.

She asks him
what he dreams.
Our children, he whispers,
as she imagines
the sons and daughters
they never had.

Later
on the stairs
she begins softly
to name them.

THE LOVE

The love that ended yesterday in Texas
crawled out of the sea
fresh-eared and barnacled,
his lashless eyes astonished
at the shook-out world
where nothing swayed or rippled
but stood one-minded and dry,
pointing forever upward.
He dressed
and boarded a slow boat
that kept him centuries adrift,
finally jumping ship
in a country shaped like a lobster,
the claws of its faraway shores
reaching out to him.
There his journey continued
like the long, slow haul
of a glacier, over mountains,
through gorges and canyons,
across prairies where
ghosts of Indians
whispered his many names.
To the edge of the desert
where he bought a hat
and mounted the horse
that brought him here
to this honky-tonk,
to the corner near the jukebox
where he sits
mourning the woman
whose voice, like the sea,
still calls him.

GRAVITA

Newton measured
the speed at which an object
falls to earth by rolling it
down an incline, thus slowing
into human proportions
the rate of perpetual motion.
I watched as my teacher
drew in perfect geometric design
the lines and connecting dots,
the little globe stopped
enroute down the dusty board. I don't know
how I passed the test but I understood
well why Newton died a virgin—the small
room they found him in, the pendulums,
the telescopes divesting white light
into its worldly colors.

Years later in Italy
in The Gallery of the Academy,
a young woman beneath the huge, lovely
penis of *David*. She had stumbled, was weeping.
"Gravita! Gravita!" she cried
as she hoisted herself onto an elbow,
her other arm circling her swollen belly
like a moon detached from its planet.

Outside, the olive trees were turning
their silvery spheres toward the light
and somewhere a star, though more
slowly than the apple, was falling.

I LOVE HOW MY NIECE LOVES JESUS

I love how my niece loves Jesus,
how the white testament
fits the little fold of her hand
like the purse she sometimes carries
filled with make-believe rouge and mascara.
Or the way a bean seed nestles
in the cupped palms of cotyledons.

And, yes, I love him too, I say when she asks,
imagining what it would be like—his body
falling through mine, hair listing
his shoulders like a biker's,
the good heart and tongue.
And the fall taking centuries
before we are back to where we were
when God that first difficult day cracked
like a paramecium, like an egg,
like a small ship against the rocks
whose prow and stern
now drift
toward separate edges of the world.

~~~ OLD RAIN ~~~

NAMESAKE

for Cathy Fiscus, 3, who died in an abandoned well the summer of 1949

From the face of the earth
is how they put it
when someone disappears
so all day your father paces
among bulldozers and cranes
as your mother sits in the car
muttering to the visor.

I hang in my own mother's womb,
little turtle, zeppelin of skin and marrow.
The chipped ice she craves
grinds in her teeth
like pneumatic saws.

And because television that summer
will be the closest thing to miracle,
she gives in to the sloppy recliner,
to the window fan's rattle and clack
to watch as hour by hour
hope fails in black and white.

Down there you must have heard something queer.
A scraping at earth, some ancient burrowing.
And what word can name the descent of midgets
armed with buckets and spades?

You lived two days, your voice
tamping at the surface, that one song
rising now and then into the suspended mike.

Then—air, light. The blood
hammering at the soft closure
of my skull, they lifted
me out, all slag and sediment,
sludge of another life,
and gave me your name.

Falling in Love with Sickness

After the next one was born
and mother abandoned my bed
to take up with the pink, wrinkled thing,
its eyes stuck shut with mucus,
wispy hair clotted to its head,
the small cave of its mouth
sucking out her life,
I rolled over into the warm grave her body left
and fell in love.

Flu and scarlet fever.
Diphtheria and mumps.
Then willing myself yellow,
I leaned back into the down of quilts and pillows
as jaundice crept over my body.

My limbs racked and shuddered with chills, glowed
with fever's bright hallucinations,
erupted in sores and ulcers,
those rare jewels of dog days
glistening against my skin.

I licked my tongue into the sugar bowl
lapping up the forbidden grains,
the sweet promise of diabetes,
and imagined my mother
easing the daily needle into my skin.

I dreamed of steamy jungles,
malaria riding on the wing and buzz of insects.
Waded in filthy ponds
hunting that old frog typhus,
the charmed prince of stagnation
longing for my kiss.

Coughed, wheezed, and vomited
until Mother came back to my bed,
fluffing pillows,
bearing bowls of grapes and oranges,
that warm jar of mentholatum
she rubbed into my chest,
quieting the small animal that rattled there.

One by one she drove them all away,
each walking out of my life
like a friend she did not approve of.
When she went back to her ironing,
to the pots boiling on the stove,
the dirty floors,
to the whimpers and cries of that other one
who had mastered some chronic ailment,

I dragged myself from bed and slowly dressed, pausing
to breathe the last sweet smells
of the sickroom, then turning
stepped quietly through health's lonely door.

Asthma

The walls, like thunder,
threaten to move in closer.

Her mother has rubbed a poultice
into her skin.
Her chest is that heavy fish
her brother pulled
from Bender's Creek in June.
A frying pan.
Fat cat too old to move.

The air is a bubble
that drifts above her mouth,
a rainbow window on each side
like the one you catch again
upon the ring you blew it from
and hold for one last moment.

Mornings
she can see from her high window
children playing
on the banks below,
their laughter like frantic birds
beating against the sill.

They tug and pull
at one another's hands,
at pockets, belts and cuffs
each in his own small need
to drag the other down

to become king of the hill
higher than the trees,
the chimney tops,
higher than the clouds
where she believes
there must be air enough
for even her.

MARKINGS

Besides the many rituals utilizing various kinds of markings, a mother
might cure an asthmatic child by marking her height with a green reed.

These markings on the wall
might mean the nights
a mother counted home her son
or the things she could have said
to make him stay.

First one mark. Then another.
Two more. And now a slash across
them all makes five. And then
five hundred. Until the county
threw the woman out. Left the wall
that marked the history of her grief.

When I was ten my mother
held my back against the northern wall,
the one that shook each time
the train came through.

Make sure the reed is green,
and from the water's edge, she'd say—
and the child's back flush to the wall.

Mark her height precise
and careful as the dress you'd cut
to please the mayor's wife.

Make sure it's spring
and when the child has grown
beyond the mark, note
how her breath has eased.

We women know this art
like a lover's face we might
have traced so lightly as he slept,
marked each feature as if our hands

could memorize the high cheek bones,
firmness of the chin.

We pass it down, this need
to validate the things
we did or did not do,
said or should have said.

Still, there's something in it.
The woman who took up weaving
knows the wall's still there.
I breathe against a pane of glass
and cannot see my breath.
And on nights so long
the moon becomes a man I cannot stand,
I cup my palms and almost see your face.

MEN

The summer I was ten
my mother fell in love with Elvis.
I watched her swoon into the TV set
moaning Love Me Tender to the screen,
my father's supper burning on the stove.
One morning she combed
the cotton from her hair,
packed a canvas bag
and took the train to Memphis.
When she came back
I asked where Elvis was
and she cried for days.

Men! I remember her saying years later,
me sixteen and broken-hearted
by a boy across the tracks
whose name I never knew.
Morning until dusk
I walked the brooding rails.
Through June and through July
and into August
until summer loaded up and left
the way a yard sale closes down at dark,
the racks of faded dresses hauled back in.

We both survived.
That boy moved away to Kansas
and the county covered up the tracks
with pitch and tar.
Father took Mother back
and never mentioned Elvis.
And mother never burned his food again
nor sang.

THE GIRL WHO DROVE THE NAIL

August and you're ten again.
In the elbow tree's crook of arm
you sit all day and watch
as air sags
like heavy hives of bees
dreading winter.

And it is the time
when mother left,
her thin frame
rippling with the heat
in that strange way
heat rises
from tracks in summer.

Your eyes see distances
never known before,
grow dim,
retrace to where a turtle
hauls across the ties
something vague
and heavy as a planet.

Through an older wound
the nail drives quick
into the patterned back
deep into design
past heart
through gut
to stone.

He grows into the tracks
like nothing's changed.
Moon lugs night across the sky.
Rivers, whole forests learn.

THE SHELTER

for my grandfather

Sun, July, could send us scuttling
for the saving hole
you'd dug for us.
October blew dry leaves
across the top like rats
where far below we thought
their scratchings bombs.
You taught us what we needed.
How to add the cans and jars
divided by the number who survived.
Our spelling words were
aerial and *bombardment*
and the two we never could pronounce—
Hiroshima, Nagasaki.

No matter. What bomb
could find us there?
What death, when all along
those muddy walls grew jars
of beans and corn we lifted
to their shelves like porcelain dolls.
The war we waited for refused to come.
Still, you taught us well
the rudiments of breaking ground.
When we climbed out
the sky still looked the same.
The silo held the sun up like a prize.
The spotted cow, who'd watched
as we went down, looked up
indifferent as the clover on her tongue.

ELEGY FOR MY BROTHER

You joked it was devil's shoestring
that you sowed,
not oats,
but poppy, larkspur, clover,
your pollen floating everywhere
to towns so far away they had no names,
to a war where you died
though they sent you back alive,
the brilliant map of your body
the work of skilled cartographers
whose faces you never even saw.

Hot.
It was so hot there,
you awakened one night screaming,
the ice I brought to cool your fever
melting into rivulets
on your brow
until the cold transferred us laughing

to the summer
Mama's Frigidaire blew up
and every morning
you were sent for ice
from the plant across the creek,
that one huge block a day
you dared bring back by way of stepping stone.

I watched from the edge of our back yard
as you emerged from the mouth
of the ice plant
lugging that heavy block
like a sleeping child,

how once on the curved, slick surfaces
you balanced like a circus star
above the creek's shallow death
pretending now and then to lose your footing
until I wept and laughed at the water's edge
then cheered you on to safety.

The fever eased. You slept
and dreamt, as I imagined,
your scattered seed children:
what strange countries' meadows
they frolic through,
the wreaths of poppy, larkspur,
devils' shoestring
circling their delicate heads;

what waters they linger towards
like rats after some faint note
that in another time and place
might have come close to music;

what darkness they tightrope over,
bearing your heart inside them
like ice.

THE COMPASS

When Father finally packed his bag and left
one Sunday after Mother called him a derelict,
I looked up the word in Funk and Wagnalls
and finding that it meant an abandoned ship,
thought how alike we were. Always dreaming
of traveling. Free. Sailing out of that dirty
millyard. Columbus and Vespucci, searching
some secret passage. Lands of spices. Diamonds,
gold and silver. The startled natives
bowing as if we were gods. Next day

in science class, Mr. Hanson gave each of us
a compass to keep, tried to teach us north,
south, east and west. But when he said the compass
always pointed north, my face fell. I glared
at him the rest of the period, wondering
who in his right mind would always want to go
north. An uncle had been there, had warned me
about the place where they mug you in broad
daylight, talk funny, don't understand
real English. I took the compass

home and put it in a drawer beneath the gown
my mother was saving
for when she died. That night I dreamed
of China and Rome, those pink and orange
countries in my geography book, flat paper mountains
my fingers could easily climb, oceans
calm beneath the safe ship of my hand. In the middle

of the night, when I got up to pee, I found my father
slumped, a sunken steamer, across the couch, his suitcase
leaning against the table like a terrible anchor. I

went back to bed, clutching the compass
I had dug from the bottom of the drawer, its smooth glass
sweating in my hand like a flattened globe, and changed
my mind, began planning that slow journey north.

BONE

We became addicted to chaos after years of living in the midst of trauma.
—from a "Laundry List" for children of alcoholics

Our house was a needle's eye
you shoved a camel through.
You gave us each a bone.
Arm finger toe and ankle
to be tucked in childhood's baggage
and lugged around from day to day
as if always we waited
to board some invisible train.
When you finally died
we were surprised
at the benignancy of doors,
passivity of pots and pans,
the incipient incipience.
The quiet you left
hunkered in corners
like sacks of tongueless kittens.
For a while we kept our distance,
trying hard to love the silence
then one by one
we gathered with our sticks
and began to poke.

ROSIE, OLD RAIN

Suddenly, out of the chronic cyclone
of our parents' arguing
she would spin, tiny dervish
from their center, tapping
and whirling across the linoleum
to the kitchen table
where she would climb
amid the bowls of beans and okra.
And nothing we had seen on *Wild Kingdom*
came close to that hair
spuming out like foam
her elbows and wrists
furious as the hinged skinny legs
of shadow puppets, small shaman
dancing the devils out.
And always Mother, stunned into distraction,
would turn to scold and lift her down
as Father slunk sobering from the room.

Sometimes, hours after lightning, hard wind.
When quiet and the swayed trunks of pines
have righted themselves again
there arises the slightest breeze
and we are called from the debris and broken limbs
to the tops of trees where, listen, somewhere
in the branchy green sphere between sky and earth
there is the dance of old rain raining.

~~~ LOSSES ~~~

LOSSES

Each morning, as sun calls back
from the grass its lent vapors,
that crew of little spirits rising for work,
my retriever begins his ritual of cheeps and chirps
like a nest of sparrows or those biddies
parents buy at Easter for their children
knowing they will die. He won't soil his pen,
so by the time I've had my coffee
and staggered to the yard to let him out,
he is desperate, bolts through the gate
and across the path he has worn in our lawn.
He circles and circles, sniffing out
the perfect spot, lifts his leg, then lopes,
as he was trained, into the woods,
to the sweet mulchy floor of pine and cedar.
Again he sniffs, circles, then curves
his tail-end under like a giant hook or comma.
The Muslim in him faces east
where the scarab sun climbs the sky's moist web.

It doesn't seem right, watching him.
Hunched like an aborted fetus. Straining.
His legs trembling. His soft eyes
averted from my insensitive gaze. The way one summer
in Indonesia, that woman, bathing
beneath the ashy rise of Gunung Agung,
turned shyly away as our cameras continued to click.
She had waded, naked, with her youngest to the bank
where he stooped like a little frog, emptying
his bowels onto the sand. Was it then I knew
I would never have children? Could not bear
at so close a range those leaks
and solvents. Would get instead a dog
I could train to go off into the woods
carrying deep into shadow the body's chronic losses.

Salt

Bane of slugs. Saviour
whiter than the snow and ice
it melts in winter
clearing roads and sidewalks,
swelling gutters to rivers of salty sludge.
Moniker for sailors
who watch from the wharf on Saturdays
or haul, each summer, to the Cuttysark
carloads of grandchildren
dreaming instead of Disney World.
And when my grandfather began
the slow sloughing off into death,
it was the first to go.

In Grandmother's pantry, rows
and rows of jars shattered light
like a rose window. Everything
good—smoked, cured, or pickled.
Quarts of sauerkraut, scarlet medallions of beets.
Peaches, those vinegary sweet yolks
she slithered from a spoon into our mouths.

As we salted the starry centers of apples
Grandmother's bread rose like a soft moon
and she told bible stories
to horrify us into goodness. The snakes,
the floods we had somehow missed, the disobedient
woman turned to salt.

And what did Grandfather mean,
who, in the next room, kept mumbling
not worth his salt, about the migrant
Grandmother had hired to run the farm?

So he ate his last meals bland
and talked of salt
the way an old man remembers lovers
long since gone to rags and toothless.

TO A FRIEND WITH A HYPHENATED NAME, AFTER HER DIVORCE

Because neither name
made commotion enough to matter,
you jammed it there
like a doorstop
between the bed and bath
of love's vacation house
and kept them both.

Stay! Stay! you cried
pointing your finger
and like a good dog
it whimpered once
and lay down.

Now, it is an orphan
left on your backporch step.
It has lost its sweetness.
It has lost its teeth.

It pokes about those empty rooms
like your grandmother's old nose.
Stake without a garden.
Length of firewood that will not burn.

Little amputee,
mutation with no thumb
trailing your name like a proffered hand
no one wants to shake.

When the moon is full
it is your broomstick.
You make your rounds,
an item as they say,
cackling through the night
at your own bad joke.

When dawn brings you home
you lay it down beside you
in the dark.

To My Nephew, Age 11, of His Estranged Father

At first you will dress him
in beggar's rags
and bring him home.
And after twenty years,
unlike the dog
so old his ragged heart gave out,
you will pit him, bow in hand,
against two hundred warriors.

Or you will find him
one day in history class
stepping down from a flashing cockpit
and off the screen
to walk the projected beam
like a magic runway
into the room,
cradling his battered helmet
like a son

and you, startled into waking,
will not care
what war has brought him here.

Soon, he will be the lineman
you watched in secret
all that August day

as faceless voices snapped
then died among the wires
in his hands.

Or just the taxi driver
eating his peanuts
through the empty streets.

You know where
he would take you
and still
you want to go.

THE CURE

for Beth Couvillion, 1954-1989

Long after I thought
I had done with grieving
there arose in my chest
between the sternum and clavicle
a soft commotion, like the gerbils
caged in my niece's room
that race all night across the furious wheel.
It would start when I least expected—
in the theater during credits
or among the squash and spinach
of the produce aisle. My breath
would catch, my hand flutter to that spot
the way a mother's hand
rises instinctively to her child's brow
as if touch itself could bring the fever down.

Anxiety attacks, my doctor said,
scribbling in hieroglyphics his perfect cure.
I took the pills, and sure enough
the palpitations stopped, packed up and moved
like a band evicted from the premises.
But I found I missed
that little tuning up of cymbals and drums
the way I still missed you
and threw the pills away.

COMMUTE

The year my father was dying my mother
fell in love. Evenings, after my drive from
the hospital, she would call, who years before
had fled the minefield of our home,
to talk as if we were girls, her voice beating
like wings in the bad connection. And
she would speak of strange clamorings
beneath her skin. Something rising—parturient.
A soft ruckus of spears and drums
as if the little lost tribe of her sex had
stumbled suddenly into sun.
I dreaded that commute between the living and dead
to where my father lay, the impotent
machine humping the fagots of his lungs.

The Watch

Between the time the doctors
switched off the life machine
and you died
I watched how my brothers
in those fifteen minutes
touched every part of your body,
you who had never touched them.
And I saw how they went at you,
grazing the pale lichens of your skin,
the wet mouths of bedsores,
their foreheads tensed
like the brows of small boys
examining their dog for ticks.

And then they were under sheets,
their hands kneading the dumb blue
box of your chest, pocked ankles and shins
the spent penis that shot
the sperm we wriggled out of.
I felt suddenly shy watching like that,
your sons, after all those years,
having their way with you.

THIRD FLOOR WEST

Even after the heart and breath lines
on the screen above my father's head
went straight as the lines down highways
that separate the coming from the going,
one eye refused to close, kept staring
into the room, green and slippery as a beached fish.
My brother kept passing his hand in front of it
the way coroners in old westerns
test the dead for reflex. A film
covered the dark pupil, the iris
pale and swimmy as the yolk of an egg.
At intervals my brother would walk away
to fumble the leaves of the philodendron
some relative had sent, and then return
to ask again where the doctor was,
why he had not come to close it.
Finally a nurse appeared, and to calm my brother
placed her hand flat against my father's brow
and eased her thumb across the lid
like a woman drawing shades in a small house
long after the lights are out.

Fire

After he died, my mother told
how once my father set fire
to the closet where my sisters and I kept our clothes.
It was a day in September, too early
for that odd angle of light that signals fall,
too cool for a Carolina summer, as if
October had seeped from its proper space
in the feed-store calendar behind the stove, bleeding
through to the page above, to the quiet
bowed heads of September's elk and bison.

We were thumping doodlebugs
across the cool, damp earth beneath the porch
and she was in the kitchen kneading bread
when she smelled smoke coming from the room
where we slept. She ran with the sticky milk
and flour oozing between her fingers. She ran
like a woman flaming, mad through the burning doors
of an asylum some psycho set fire to.
And there he was, my father, in the closet
curled on his hands and knees like a lone camper
beating out the campfire's rampant blaze.

For the insurance money, he told her later
when she asked why he had done it.
He wouldn't have let it hurt us, he said,
or the rest of the house,
just a few old clothes we could no longer wear.
We were in bed asleep and she wanted to kill him.
To pummel the mouth and nose the way she had found him
hunkered, slapping at his pathetic flame.
But all she did was take him to her breast
and hold him, shaking her head,
saying Edward, Edward.

THE BOXERS

When my father, after twenty years, came home
to die, circling, circling, like an animal
we believed extinct, it was my crazy aunt
who took him in, who told later
how the taxi had dumped him
bleached and whimpering on her porch.
And she who had not lived with him
thought his sons and daughters cruel
not to come when he began to call our names.

He died, and soon after, a package in brown wrapping
arrived at my address. My sister, who did not
attend the funeral, kept urging me to open it
and I kept saying I would, soon. Every day
when I came home from work, there it was
sitting at my back door, the remnants
of my father's life—years in the mill
spinning and doffing, then drinking into morning
as he railed at the walls, the cotton
still clinging to his fists. Weeks had passed

when finally my sister and I, after two stiff bourbons,
began to rip the paper, slowly in strips
like archaeologists unclothing a mummy.
And all that was there were a few plaid flannels,
the jacket to a leisure suit, and a pair of boxers,
white and baggy, Rorschached in urine—a smaller
size, my sister said, than the way she remembered him.
Then she offered to drop the things at the Salvation Army
store she passed on her way home. In July

we went shopping for swim suits and I could
see her in the curtained stall across from mine.
She was pulling her slip over her head when I saw
she was wearing them, her thighs like the pale stems
of mushrooms emerging from the boxers' billowy
legs, whiter, softer now, washed clean. I still

can't say why my sister, that day in the Salvation
Army store, glanced up, as I've imagined,
to see if anyone was watching

before she slipped those boxers from the soiled heap
of our father's clothes. Nor why
I took so long to open that package, both wanting
and fearing whatever lay inside. Like a child
huddled by the campfire who cries out in terror
at the story someone just told
and, still weeping, begs for it again.

~~~ THUNDER ~~~

FALL

On a day when the world has just begun
to pack it all in,
the earth luxuriant with decay,
mushrooms littering the ground
like golfballs
some boy has resurrected for money,
I catch sight of my husband
from the upstairs window
where I am hanging curtains.

His broad back is turned to me
where he stands at the edge of the garden
and although he is not a religious man
he holds his hands in front of him
clasped low like someone praying.
His face tilts toward the sky,
toward the baring ash and maple,
the dogwoods clotted with autumn berries.
His head turns slowly from side to side
and I imagine his eyes are closed
as in the last unearthly moments of love.
Then I see that he is pissing.

Squirrels and chipmunks scatter.
A flock of starlings has risen
to the highest limbs of the sweetgum
and the dog retreats
to the safety of the woodpile
as the torrent spatters
onto shriveled bean vines,
parched okra, the shrunken heads
of cabbage. And in the room above

I am thinking, This is what it's like
to be a man caught between luck and ruin.
Like my father the night the mill shut down.
How I found him there in the coalyard
where long chutes disappeared into the spinning room,
the cotton clinging like angel hair
to his Adam's apple.
As starlight rode the beautiful arc of his urine
onto the gleaming coalpile
I stood in the shadow of the smokestack
watching him do
the very worst a good man can do,
the curses catching in his throat
like bad machinery:
piss on it piss on it piss on it.

THE FAT LADY TRAVELS

On any train
she is the occupant
of either seat.
No hopes for a handsome stranger.
No petty arguments
as to who
will get the window
or the aisle.
She gets them both.

When she dreams
she is never the goddess
turning men to pigs.
She is the pig.
She is the one gross eye
of the Cyclops
fending off the spears
of her disgrace.

She is all of Brobdingnag.

Her green dress blowzes
in the halcyon wind.
She is turgid water
flooding the station,
home for leviathans.

What she should lose
would be enough
to make the sister
she never had.

And how thin
the both of them would be
gliding on fine-point skates
across some fragile pond

and, oh, it holding!

SETTING THINGS STRAIGHT

*Actual insanity is apt to be shown in a sharp change in the habitual way of writing.
The slovenly writer becomes neat and precise and the careful writer begins to be
almost totally illegible.*
                              —Mumford's *Graphology*

Her eyes migrate, she thinks,
like the ugly fish
that always, eyes-side-up,
mistakes the sky for home.

She thinks the minutes months.
Morning, June, she walks
a garden path toward late November
where the carcass of a scarecrow sleeps.
The ground she'd hoped
to gather supper from
lies hard and fallow.

Empty basket heavy as the moon,
she turns in fear that home again
an April scent of green
could mangle her.

She wants the planets
all in place once more,
the moon and stars aligned.

One day in early spring,
the morning long,
she tries to imitate
her girlhood alphabet

each *o* precise and round
as the angel's mouth
that lolled for months
above the tinsel and the lights
then toppled from its brittle height
to where,
like snakeskins,
ribbons curl beneath a tree
that should by now have been
first flame, then smoke, air,
and memory.

THIRD CHILD

There is no such thing as a dyad, only remnants of an excluded third.
—Carl Whitaker

You have to believe it would have been the one
to save you all. The miscarriage. The abortion.
Or the night between the mill's last whistle
and your mother's freshly powdered skin,
your father chose instead to count stars all night
as if counting, like a poultice
against the sky's dark wound,
would draw them down.

Your mother went to sleep
mad as a moon-ridden woman, her womb
shutting down like the mill when times
were hard, your father laid off again.

It might have been a sister.
One who would have let you wear her clothes.
Crinolines. Pearl-studded collars.
You would have learned together
what to do with hair, the secrets
of eye shadow, bright lipsticks.
And when the blood began its journey down your legs,
you would have knelt together
in the locked toilet, arms about each other
warding off the death it must have meant.

Or a second brother.
A good one this time.
Face too soft for battering.
Heart so sweet it would have gathered
the broken family in
the way street people, wintering,
migrate from under bridges,
from out of bags and boxes
to huddle about a flaming bin.

SAVIOURS

My father had one saviour, booze.
And though I hated the old breath
rank as that rabid hound
he cornered one afternoon
in the blinding forsythia,
the shot ringing out
as we watched the crazed thing
leap once into the air
and then touch down
spinning like a small tornado
in the red Carolina dust,
I had to admire his consistency.

It was you, Mother, I couldn't forgive
after you walked out on Jesus
then flitted for years like a lost angel
from one saviour to another.

How you wept all one summer
for Michelangelo,
each morning at breakfast
planning the pilgrimage
you would one day take
to that chapel where his spirit
still floated, you said,
in the steep dome
for lack of a better place.

I pretended to listen
as I ate my oatmeal
and thought of Nancy Owens.
Once on the schoolyard swing

I watched her long legs
shove backwards against the dirt
then swing forward, pushing out and up
higher and higher
until she was touching the sky,
her toes pointing toward heaven

where she hovered for a moment
then, the long chains looping the bar,
came down in a swell of dust.

The winter you went back
to Jesus, an estranged wife
lugging your heavy suitcases,
I thought of that day
Nancy Owens left earth
and then, before my eyes,
came back alive,
the long smooth arc of her body
dark against the sky,
something I had seen and could believe in.

WATCHING FOR HALLEY'S COMET IN THE YORK COUNTY PLANETARIUM AT 3:00 A.M., APRIL 7, 1986

Like that date I knew in high school
it doesn't show.
Like Jesus, after the long
shadowy drowning when I was twelve,
my face crushed
beneath the preacher's hand
that finally after years
dragged me flailing and coughing
to the river's edge, to the towel
that hung like a saviour
across my mother's arm.

The sky still empty twenty years later,
we sit beneath the domed ceiling of the planetarium
bright with artificial stars, as the amateur
astronomer points with his luminated stick
to the spot where it would be
if the clouds miraculously parted
and the comet blazed across the heavens
like the children of Israel.

He dances embarrassed
across the dome of our disappointment,
lids of our groggy eyes as we drift
in and out of sleep, catching his random words:

Scorpius and *Mars*. *Taurus* and *Perihelion*.
Then in his trembling voice
something about last night,
how right off 77 from the window
of his truck, it bloodied the entire sky.

And again I am a schoolgirl
trying hard to believe
what the eye cannot see.
Like years ago, tenth grade,

my end-of-semester science report,
how from memory, that vague
affair of the heart I had learned to count on,
I rattled off before the entire class
everything there was
not to know about Venus.
How there the lightning flashes
and thunder rolls incessantly,
the atmosphere so thick
a person might swim right through.

I pointed with a long stick
at a chart my teacher
had suddenly pulled from nowhere,
an attic of visual aids
filled with documented sightings,
foil comets,
bright charts of constellations.

Some secret place in the ceiling
where dates could be pulled
like rabbits out of hats
and men coaxed from the dead
at a moment's notice,
amazing the eye,
staving off the heart's suspicions
for a little while.

AFTER READING IT IS ONLY A MYTH THAT A PERSON LOOKING UP FROM THE BOTTOM OF A WELL IN THE MIDDLE OF THE DAY CAN SEE STARS

I say, whoever decided that has never been there.
Listen. I was a schoolgirl just trying
to avoid recess's lonely corridors
where I had stood four days in a row
amidst an orgy of lockers
watching Susan Jones and Tommy Hough
feel each other up.

So, on Friday when the bell rang,
feigning an odd obsession for logarithms,
I talked Miss Hodgins into leaving me alone
in that dusty room filled with algebra books, tools
of perfect calculation,
the long skinny legs of compasses rigid and spread
that somehow made me need for once in my life
a schoolroom any color but green.

I jammed a stick of red chalk
into the hinged leg of Miss Hodgin's giant compass
and in minutes marked up the room
with hundreds of red circles,
their bright arcs overlapping like arms and legs
across tops of desks, across blackboards
filled with immaculate equations, across
floor and walls until the room was a bloody web
and me hanging out the window screaming, my head
and torso wedged in the slanted pane.

That's how I got there.
Down. Flip-flopping over the rim
like a too-small fish thrown back into the water.
For months I hung just below the surface,

staring up at the curious faces who came and went.
Vague groups of two and three.
Miss Hodgins. Susan Jones and Tommy Hough.
And always some stranger in white.

All reaching down.
Their mouths remorseful and agape,
the whites of their far-away eyes
arranging themselves above
like constellations.

THE FLOWER WE COULD NOT NAME

Clematis climbs the weathered
rail we split, and seizes
all within its grasp—green
tendrils, small antennae, tenacious toed
and fingered. Clinging.
Like the boy they pulled
from the reservoir, his arms
and legs in the muscle-spasmed dark
still wrapped about the oar
that must have meant such promise:
hold tight tight
tight and I will save you.

Last fall, a gift my mother sent,
a burlap sack full of bulbs
she'd thinned from her own neurotic yard.
I dumped them out, palmed each one
and named them like good children
destined to make something of themselves,
who come home each year to make us proud.

Cluster of small wombs, exotic
as their names: Desert-Candle,
Tiger Flower, Star-of-Bethlehem.

Onions with a hank of hair, witch's
head or squid: Narcissus, Hyacinth.

And these like small dried fruits
all wrinkled in their skins:
Eranthus and Anemone.

But the one we could not name,
that lay twisted, small tumor
at the bottom of the sack,

nuzzled its way somehow
into November's cold layer
and, in April's punctual thaw,
pushing its head
through the indiscriminate earth,
came anyway.

MATING SEASON ON FIRETHORN POND

In a Buddhist temple in Malaysia
I saw enclosed in glass
a shell broad as a man's hand,
smooth, orbicular saucer,
and bubbled up from the pearly surface,
seven perfect baby Buddhas
small as pencil erasers,
their diapered groins
resting in lotus position

and read how long ago
a farmer scavenging the coral reefs
was drawn to the shell's slivery beauty,
how later in the temple
monks bowed each day, chanting over it
until one by one
tiny Buddhas began to rise
like blisters under scalded flesh.

Here, geese cruise in
like carloads of pubescent boys
mad for the down of necks
while along the weedy perimeter
water fizzes in microscopic sex. I drink
wine from the bottle, flop
my white feet over the edge of the pier
and watch a muskrat trail his mate,
tail of a coonskin cap,
fat cat-o-nine scudding her wrinkled way
across the pond. Three times
she bristles, rolling him
like a pine from a logging truck. I think

of monks brooding their days
over some shell, imagine
whatever god there is
prefers proliferation
the way a muskrat, rebuffed
again and again, hangs finally on,
surfing the spiny back of his love,
that sleek, tenable tail
into ecstasy.

THUNDER

My husband calls
from his month-long trip to California
still nursing the anger
he left me holding like a small child
in the dwindling window of the airport

and hears from my side of the continent
the crack of thunder.
And yes, yes
that is what he misses most
about South Carolina.

Not the dust rising
in red puffs above the corn.
Not the lakes of carp and catfish
turning deep
in their tentative dreams of flight.

But the way
when the land is long given up for dead
and farmers have disinherited the sky
for good this time
it breaks sudden and big as forgiveness.

They don't have that here, he says
as if he were speaking
of grits or Dixie Beer
or a woman
who would stand in a storm
holding the receiver to the sky.

MYSTERIES

After love
it is a game we play,
explaining the unexplainable.
Like what happens to the wax
in dripless candles.
Or why when we remember childhood
it is always summer.

And the one I think but never ask.
How day after day across five counties
you drive that old pick-up
hauling bright bins of tools,
racks of shiny utensils,
praising the virtues of your hammers and nails
as if your wares could save the world.

Tonight the mystery you give me
is how we never see
those thick slabs of tire
when they tear away from the rims of semis,
from the rims of eighteen wheelers,
the way the soul must leave the body
dying in its sleep.
But always there they are
in the fog of morning,
collapsed on the edge of the freeway
like fallen angels.

I turn to offer my explanation,
but already you are sleeping
and I can only guess
why your face still smiles:
Good love.
Because the bolts and lags
of another month
have again equaled our second mortgage.

Because all night in your dreams
heaven and earth hang level on their hinges,
their rafters held high and sturdy.

Like the reason
that inscrutable beast the camel
smiles his mysterious smile:
because in all the world
there are ninety-nine names for God
and only he knows the hundredth.

HANGING THE SCREENS

August. Sunday. In the distance
a congregation of thunderheads
like heavy nuns enroute to Mass
and because the thing I love most
is to sit in my study during a storm,
the windows up, curtains billowing
like muses above my typewriter,
my husband decides he will hang the screens
our builder never got around to.

We own no ladder, so he hauls the screens
upstairs where he lifts himself
backwards through the window,
head and shoulders out, legs in,
wrapped tight around my waist to anchor him
while he nails the silver brackets to the outside frames.

His arms are damp with sweat
and his torso trembles as he leans out
like a telephone repairman strapped to a pole,
trusting his climbing belt, his gaffs digging
into creosote, his head poking
through networks of wires and voices.

From the road a passerby might marvel
at the back of half a man emerging
from a window and inside, a woman
grasped close to the sill—
a position no missionary would take.

Or my husband's mother walking in,
as usual unannounced, would find us there,
would pale at the sight of her son
and that woman he married, entangled in lust.

He reaches for a bracket as the rain begins
and I'm thinking of Marcy Halle's tombstone
circa 1710:

> *Here lies one whose life threads cut asunder.*
> *She was struck dead by a clap of thunder.*

What better way to go than this—
clasped in my husband's thighs high above earth,
knowing how the legend will grow:
years later, tourists lining the sidewalk,
cupping hands over their children's ears, whispering
how once a man and a woman died making love
in that window, oblivious to the storm,
the charged particles converging
like flocks of yellow birds
until their bodies glowed
and lightning became their dying faces.

TRAVELING IN TIME OF DANGER

For my brothers and sisters: Trisha, Gary, Rosie, Allen,

and Paul

October 26, 1958 – November 26, 1997

The Secret
of this journey is to let the wind
blow its dust all over your body,
to let it go on blowing,
to step lightly, lightly
all the way through your ruins,
and not to lose
any sleep over the dead, who surely
will bury their own
don't worry.

—James Wright

~~~ MOTHER LAND ~~~

SPONGES

I bought two sponges
from a woman in Tarpon Springs.
A friend had rented a car
to drive me there
through banyan and orange grove,
the waxy frangipani,
bawdy as whores, through
the wild, throaty
lushness of hibiscus,
to the graying dock
where evening fishermen
held high for the curious
crowds their glittering catch.
And there she was, moving
from basket to basket,
enumerating for the indifferent
browsers the many possibilities
of sponge. This one for dishes.
This for marble and wood.
And, oh, these for the body,
for breast and arm and thigh,
for ankle and shin. Her face glowed
and her finger trembled
as she pointed to the delicate
layers, the thousand cells
through which once flowed
the salty current. And I saw
the deep pores of her own hands
through which she too had begun
the slow emptying. Saw with what love
she held them for our inspection
turning each toward the light,
those many vacant chambers.

WOMEN DANCING WITH BABIES ON THEIR HIPS

We had traveled to that old coast,
six hours to New Bern, the long ferry
from Cedar Island to Okracoke and then
to Roanoke where Manteo, for love
of the glittering English, killed Wanchese,
and so began, even from within,
that long, slow clearing.

And that night, tourists sick
of the bloody ending of our beginning,
we went for beer and music
on the deck of the Jolly Roger
where in the starry distance
lighthouses stayed the blown
shoals of islands like paperweights.

It was there we saw them, their separate
bodies swaying among the couples
coupling on the dance floor, two women,
alone, dancing with babies on their hips,
weaving in and through, stitching up
the random piece-goods of the night.

They were banners. Their hair
starfish lit. Their faces the blossomy
bright shock of sand dollars
when you find them whole.

How useless our wondering the whereabouts
of their men, imagining them away,
some war they did not belong in,
or too late back from the shrimping boat,
and tired, to join them here. These women,
their strong lovely hips dipping
and cresting, their babies' heads
flung back in a whirl of toothless
laughter, loving the lone ride,
their wild, dumb entry into the world.

MOTHER LAND

I pitied the other children
their skinny mothers. Nothing to burrow
when the church pew began to harden
like sugar-brittle or God. Their elbows
sharp as crags we climbed to the bluff
where Jimmy Adams took our dare
and jumped and never came up again. I pitied
them their mothers, all point and longitude,
tentative as sandbars the chain gang
dozed to stay the river banks. My mama

was a continent, *terra softa*
where she sprawled in her big chair
or across the bed when thunder ripped
the shingles and rain swelled the sills
like ripe earth. And there in the valleys
of blankets and pillows, each of us staked claim
to whatever fleshy region we had chosen to settle
while the storm spent itself. My sisters
nestling the soft slopes of her breasts, me floating
meridians of hip and thigh. My mama
was promised land and we, small redoubts
not even our father could penetrate, odd denizen

from that country of men we could see
mounting the horizon, their bright
flags flying, their cannons aimed.

SNOW

It was the only act of intimacy
I ever witnessed between them—that joke
my father told her, his opening
line...*I hope it snows so deep*...and then
how, for the punch, he reached out
and pulled her to him, to whisper words
that sent her red and slapping
at his khaki shirt and then her hand
lifting to his chin to remove
the little ghosts of cotton
that fluttered there. Our teachers
had sent us home from school calling
See you Monday that Thursday in December
as we ran crazed into the schoolyard
and to our separate houses
to hold vigil for that white coming,
that promise we wanted so badly to believe
we could feel, already in the graying
sky, its soft descent. All evening
the heater roared its warmth
into the room as we talked
of snow-cream so cold it hurt
your head, the fine spin a hubcap gives
down a hill of white. But by the close
of second shift, all that had shown
was a stray, barking beneath
the streetlight, our father in from the mill,
blowing the night from his hands
and telling that joke, his mouth burrowing
into the smell of our mother's hair,
and somewhere, breaking dim above the smoke stacks,
a few odd stars no one would admit to seeing.

THEM

Jews and niggers, my father
walking in from work
or glancing up from the daily news
would shake his head and mumble
though no verb or adjective followed or preceded
to help distinguish his blessing from his curse.

I had seen one of each. Annie
in the lunchroom where I went to school
who scraped beans and carrots
from our trays into the slop,
while Abram—strange immigrant
from some place we could not pronounce—
shoveled coal into the furnace far below.
At recess we could see him near the chutes
turned, from his labour, almost black as Annie.
We held our distance, as father had warned,
and afternoons sat full in our warm desks
keeping our perfect letters inside their lines.

One day we saw the two of them
talking in that safe space
between the garbage cans and school.
We had gathered at the window
to watch a bluejay
terrify from tree to tree an owl
that even from our small view
seemed not to belong quite there
the clumsy head, heavy hook of its body
dragging air
as if sky were a river
where someone had recently drowned.

GROCERIES

I had a boyfriend once, after my mother
and brothers and sisters and I
fled my father's house, who worked
at the Piggly Wiggly where he stocked
shelves on Fridays until midnight
then drove to my house to sneak me out,
take me down to the tracks by the cotton mill
where he lifted me and the quilt I'd brought
into an empty boxcar. All night
the wild thunder of looms. The roar of trains
passing on adjacent tracks, hauling
their difficult cargo, cotton bales
or rolls of muslin on their way
to the bleachery to be whitened, patterned
into stripes and checks, into still-life gardens
of wisteria and rose. And when the whistle
signaled third shift free, he would lift me
down again onto the gravel and take me home.
If my mother ever knew, she didn't say, so glad
in her new freedom, so grateful for the bags
of damaged goods stolen from the stockroom
and left on our kitchen table. Slashed
bags of rice and beans he had bandaged
with masking tape, the labelless cans,
the cereals and detergents in varying
stages of destruction. Plenty
to get us through the week, and even some plums
and cherries, tender and delicious,
still whole inside the mutilated cans
and floating in their own sweet juice.

THE PROPOSAL

Each Christmas my brother
gathers us around in the tinseled
light of our mother's house
and kneels at the feet of the newest
woman in his life and with the flair
of men in old movies
asks her to marry him. He is aging
handsome, his pale hair receding
at his temples, the lines radiating
from his eyes like tiny oriental fans
opening into the narrowing heat
of his life. Each woman is more beautiful
than the last and younger, though it is
us he turns his face to
as he proclaims the redundant litany
of his love. We smile. Applaud
his happiness so brief we can see it washing
from his face the way a restless ghost
passes through the flesh of the living.
The way years ago, after the cranberries
and turkey, the bright wrapping
curling like discarded veils amid the flames,
we could see our father's face darken
as he began to weep. All afternoon he would weep
where he sat at the periphery
of our muted play, my sisters soothing
their tongueless dolls, my brother
grinding into the floor
the wheels of his new train.

My Father's Last Wish

When they called me from the hospital
to say you had slipped into a coma
I told them, though you had requested
otherwise, to plug you back
into the machinery of this life
and I would hold you hostage
the way you held us all those years,
prisoners of your bitterness and rage.

And I would pace at your bedside, amid
the bottles and wires and tubes
the way on drunk nights you staggered
from room to room, setting each naked bulb
ablaze as your wife and children
watched, hidden, from the floorboard of the car.

And when I was good and ready, when I
had tired of rubbing the yellow
lamp of your body—forty years worth—I
would be the one to tell the doctors when.
The way, deep into those nights, it was I
who walked quietly through the rooms
of that big house, turning
all the lights you'd left burning
out.

THE BILL

When I received the bill,
Father, for your death,
statement of goods
and services rendered,
I took up my calculator
and began ticking in
the dollars and cents claimed
down the funeral home's
itemized account: $225
for your embalming, $63.50
for transferral of your
remains, $34.98 for your tie
and socks and underwear.

Funny how they'd referred to me
as *buyer*, they the *seller*
as if, after a long journey alone,
I had stopped by choice
at some roadside stand
to stretch and browse and select
among the many wares—tomatoes,
cantaloupe and corn, the sweet chambered
lushness of peppers, still rich
with the good black smell of earth.

I confess I didn't want to pay
but got out the pen and checkbook
anyway, signed my name
and scrawled the total in,
knowing how sometimes
we're asked to pay up twice.
Once for what we never had.
Once for when it's taken back.

A SOUTHERN RHETORIC

"It's a sight in this world
the things in this world
there are to see," my mother says
as she hurries between the stove
and Sunday table. She is just back
from vacation. Happy.
Talking mountains. Talking rivers.
Big cedars and tidal bores.
When I tease her for redundancy,
her face glows like a sturgeon moon
risen above fat buttery atolls
of biscuits, steaming promontory
of roast. She shakes her finger
in my face and scolds me good:
"Girl, don't you forget who it was
learned you to talk."

Amazing she would want
to lay claim to these syllables
piling up like railroad salvage
when I speak, to these words slow as hooves
dredging from the wet of just-plowed fields.
I watch her turn, embarrassed, to the sink,
to the pots and pans she will scrub
to a gleam so bright we can see ourselves
as if the two of us stared back
from the lost rhetoric of memory.
From the little house, the crib
where she bent each day, naming
for me the world where words always fail,
warranting, now and then,
those few extra syllables,
some things spoken twice.

KWANZAA

When I sent my uncle the Kwanzaa
Christmas card, black cubist Christ,
each angle of his visage full and visible

like the fractured-back-together-again
women of Picasso, when I sent my uncle
this card printed on recycled paper,

uncle I had been always a little
partial to, diagnosed by the State *simple
schizophrenic*, meaning not dangerous

to society or himself though dysfunctional
enough to qualify for the small check
they mailed to him each month for food

and warmth and shelter. *My salary*, he told
me once, *payment for staying out of the loony
bin* (he even—God knows—gets raises

like the rest of us every now and then.)
When I sent my uncle this card, he jumped
on his bike and pedaled to my mother's house

where the two of them shook their heads
and in quiet deliberation decided
to call a meeting. I don't know what

happened there, not having been invited,
though my sister told me she was told
everyone showed up—Aunt Juanita and Uncle

Henry. Harold and Aunt Gladys. Loma and Dub
and Willie Mae—each bearing a pot-luck
dish to be spread on Mama's table when business

was done. It was not so much the recycled paper,
she told me she was told, or the black
Christ (some of the finest people they'd ever

known—don't get them wrong—were colored.)
but those three mysterious words *Peace
and Light*, I had scribbled between the card's

generic message and my name. Told me she
was told how each in turn hugged
my mother, wrung their hands and pondered

what he or she, in my tender years, might
have done to prevent what I had come to.
Told me she was told how in the end—after

the chicken and potatoes, the biscuits, the tea
and green bean casserole, the plates and forks
put back in their proper place—they decided

there was nothing anyone could do
so let it pass. Told me she was told
how my uncle's weathered tires

rode him safely home, my card
tucked deep inside the pocket of his coat.
How the night frogs keened

a song he'd not remembered hearing.
And something   something
not quite right

about the moon

My Mother, Ralph Kramden, and God

One of these days, Alice. One
of these days! Ralph Kramden's bus-driver voice
would threaten as whole families in good-hearted

American anger shook their fists into Saturday night's
black and white glow of The Honeymooners. Outside
beneath a corrugated sky of stars, bomb shelters

flickered their snowy network across the lawns
and how sweet it was, my sister and me, after Alice
and Ralph had made up once again and our mother

and father had climbed the long separate stairs
to their beds. How sweet those wild boys we knew
were waiting at the corner of Eleventh and Elm,

their souped-up Chevy humming and sputtering
as we crawled in for the climb up Cemetery Bluff.
Later, as streetlights began their timed dying-out,

they would drop us off, our backs and thighs
a throbbing grid of coils and springs. And always,
just as we turned, quiet, onto the path leading

to our porch, certain we'd pulled it off this time,
our mother's voice, tired and other-worldly, floating
from the window above—*I'll get you, just you wait,*

tomorrow, and we imagined a ghostly fist rising
out of her sleep as if we and our little crime
existed only in the bad neighborhood of her dreams.

But by tomorrow she had somehow forgotten her threat
that seemed to drift like fallout onto our heads,
like soot from the millyard smokestack

that dirtied the laundry she had so carefully
hung. And we, like Alice, had again escaped
the Great One's wrath. That house is gone now.

Those boys. My sister cities away
and Jackie Gleason dead. Bomb shelters obsolete
as the backseats of cars, now that we die for love.

Still, who could help but wonder exactly what it was
my sister and I and Alice had night after night
escaped. Or if we had escaped at all, knowing

how the channels sometimes cross and the voices
blur—*I'll get you, just you wait, tomorrow.*
How in the truant heart that old fist still shakes.

BRINGING BACK THE DEAD

There is this little game
      my niece wants to play
            when she visits, that I played

when I was a child, that I
      taught her to play. She offers
            me her hand she has made into a fist

and I wrap my own around her wrist,
      delicate-veined, blue with the young oxygen
            of her blood, and squeeze it tight,

cutting off the circulation, though
      not enough to hurt, and with my other hand
            begin to knead and rub the knot

of palm and knuckles, dirty
      from the labor of her play. I rub
            the magic lamp of her small fist

and signal her to open, then count
      each bloodless finger one by one. Again
            she closes. I knead and rub. She opens

and I count. We repeat
      until her fingers wither, pale
            as asparagus spears the Chinese

harvest for their tenderness in the dark.
      Why is it we keep returning to this game
            she calls *bringing back the dead?*

Knowing how we fear them, trusting
      the heavy angels, the stone toes pressing.
            Stay put! they seem to warn, spreading

their wings above the fresh-turned earth.
        And always shrieks of dread
                and laughter fill the room

when at the final moment of our game,
        she opens and I count again, then reach
                into the center of her shriveled palm,

drawing my fingers upward
        as I release the grip on her wrist
                my other hand has held.

Ghost! Ghost! She squeals,
        as the blood rushes back
                and she imagines some lost spirit

swimming her body into the world again.
        I laugh and explain the principles of blood,
                physiology of artery and vein

as one day she will explain
        to her daughter, after loosening
                the grip on her wrist

and something neither of them can see
        goes rafting. And she, too, will insist
                on the likelihood of spirits,

as I, great aunt, dead
        and long forgotten, rise,
                through the wash of her tiny palm,

ignoring the blood's easy logic,
        the granite weight of angels.

STRING

"You've got a string hanging,"
my sister says, and we all
look down at my tattered leggings,
the ones I pull on—dirty or
clean—when I need something old,
some ancient softness
against the worn and calloused
sorrows of the flesh. We look down,

I, my sister, niece, and brother-in-law,
to the gray thread dangling from the hole
three quarters of the journey up my inner thigh,
in dangerous proximity to that
place—that dark crossroads
still unnameable here in the rural
South. My brother-in-law reaches

deep into the pocket of his pants
and pulls out his lighter, pretending
to ignite it like a fuse or wick.
I jump back and scream as he breaks
wild and uncontrollable into laughter,
unstoppable guttural roar of this man
who two days and two nights has not
for his just-dead father stopped crying.

Who gives in, now, to this moment,
to the odd and sudden grace of silliness,
the unpronounceable god of string.

Weather

Even the ancient Egyptians
knew God was nothing
more than weather,
a warm, dry wind
surfing the Nile's easy swell
as Osiris drove his faithful chariot
across the sky. It's why
they tried to take it with them,
lugging into their tombs
their worldly possessions—pots
and pans, tables and chairs,
and the favored servants,
gone out on the pharaoh's finest stuff.
Meanwhile, next door, the bug-eyed Sumerians
quaked between the wild, impossible surge
of the Tigris and Euphrates, dreading
the grave, fearing they might awaken
into another life of flood and storm.

It's no wonder barbers live
the longest and happiest lives.
All day that old confession of weather
passing from chair to chair
and the hum of shears
climbing the ridged and snowy slopes
of all those necks.

It's no wonder the last love
of my grandmother's life
was the weatherman on the local channel
she kept her TV tuned to, her hair
a knot of blue against her neck
as she rocked on the porch

between updates, calling out
the latest forecast to passersby.
And no wonder each would stop a moment
out of their busy lives
to listen, to smile and nod
before moving on, taking with them
that small gift of weather, that prayer.

LEARNING HOW TO PRAY

EASTER

"Orrys," Allen says and laughs
when he drips gravy from Mama's
porcelain dish onto the table.
It is Easter and we are speaking,
as we do at all our family gatherings,
the old language of childhood, the way
my niece began rolling the world
into words, dropping the initial "s"
and grafting it to the end
like an awkward branch from
some other family's tree.

So "sorry" is what he meant.
"Sorry" for the stain blossoming
brown as the tips of dogwood
on the lace cloth used only
for holidays. All day this language
more obtuse than the Rosetta Stone
as my niece cringes in her seat,
too old now, she believes, for such silliness.
She is just thirteen and waiting
for the blood to begin. "Anitarys,"
my sister whispers, speaking of the small napkin
she has begun to carry in her purse
and we laugh.

Later, because he is so far
away, we will phone our youngest brother
and how's "Ausalitos" our mother will ask
before passing the phone to each of us
who will speak to him of weather,
the profusion of daffodils lighting
the far pasture of the farm, though
no one will mention the disease
he carries inside him, a language
we can't yet speak, and no stone,
no stone to help us understand.

KINGDOM

When my brother
finally spoke its name,
the white cells of his body
having relinquished
their ancient
instruments of war
the small bombs
silenced
and the hand grenades
the tanks slow
retreat into mirage
the horses
dismounted
and the bright swords
sheathed
the sticks
the stones
laid
finally down
and the little lost
animal of the spirit
rising
stepping its soft
hooves into the light,
I wanted
to know that peace
walk into that quiet
kingdom
to lie down
in a life like that.

Sequoia

Later, arm-in-arm,
we walked through
Muir Woods, its deep
and leafy symmetry older
than history, wandered
among ferns and azaleas,
through the crags of Cathedral
Grove where he stepped
suddenly into the hollow
of a giant Sequoia
and asked me to take
his picture. His breathing
was measured and heavy
as I waited for the light
to signal the camera
ready. He smiled I clicked
and again he stepped
into the world
asking if I wanted to know
how it felt when the doctors
told him he had no T-cells
left. I nodded, keeping my eyes
averted, worrying the camera
back into its worn-out
case. Free, he said, I could
breathe again. After ten years
I could breathe. Get on
with my life.

L'Art Brut

On the fifth day of my visit,
after the sweet and heady
cruise through Napa and Sonoma,
the walk along the Castro
where the homeless sick
waited for the doors

of the Cannabis Club to open—all
legal my brother assured
me—after the starry, perforated
Big Top of the Russian River,
he asks if today I could explore
alone, shop or something,

so he might rest while his weekly
artificial fix of immunity
takes hold. So I leave
to buy scarves and end-of-season
dresses, to forage the gleaming
stalls of mackerel and sole,

and in the cooling evening return,
surprised to find him kneeling
in his back yard, making, of all things,
candles. His terrace is pocked with holes
across which the rays of yellow pencils
dangle from their centers makeshift wicks.

All day he has been pouring wax, reds
and blues and greens, the salvaged
stuff of wings now hardening in each sandy
grave. I sit on the steps and watch
as he digs the earth from around each candle,
exhuming his finished products, and I see

how, before pouring the wax, he had pressed
into the sides of each hole bright shards
of colored glass, variegated stones bejeweling
the clumsy creations I help carry inside and place
along the dimming window sill. Once in Lausanne,
after the obligatory tours of Europe's finest

museums, the apples of Cezanne, Monet's lilies,
the measured elegance of the Renaissance,
I happened upon a museum filled with works
of the terminally ill, tramps, and unschooled
visionaries. *L'art brut*, I was told, then left
to wander the shuttered rooms, touching

the impossible colors, the tortured
metamorphoses of debris and olive branch,
shell effigies, the heart's self-portraits gouged
from the rotted bark of stumps. And the cell
of a man who before he died carved every square
inch—the elaborate iconography of cathedrals

coaxed from the headboard of his
bed, the floor, the walls, the sill of his
barred door. First with his
fork. And when they took away his
fork, his spoon. And when they took away his
spoon, the handle of his

chamber pot.

ORCHIDS

No wonder my brother
in that year of his life
began peopling his cliffside home
with their strong and delicate
tenacity   began foraging
the genealogy of their loveliness
as if they were kin

ancient aphrodisiacs
aristocrats of sepal and stem
star-children of the orient   it is
this story he loves best
forgets twice he has told it
and tells again   how once

in old New Guinea   a Belgian
expedition and their native guide
startled upon a show of sweet Dendrobium
sprung from a mound of skulls
ribbony wreaths marking
the forgotten unhinged door
of fontanelle   each bloom
half bird   half spider
not quite furred breast
and breath of bumblebee

on the last morning of my visit
he called me to the mirror
by his front door   said *look*
as he lifted his shirt and stared
at his own reflection   I touched
the flesh around each lesion
as if to validate the freshly
tilled soil of his body
then looked up
past him   past me
to the mirrored space
behind us   to his quiet
anthem of orchids
whose seeds store no food
who can   if they must
survive on air

Pacific Time

It is not my brother's dying
that I fear, that perfect healing
bringing him forever home,
but those three hours that will have passed
between the Pacific Time of his leaving
and the Eastern Standard news
of that good death.

Four o'clock in Sausalito
is seven here, I might have baked
a loaf of bread, the measuring
and the sifting, the kneading with my hands
the way each evening on my last visit
I would massage his back, avoiding the welts
and lesions that would not heal.

I know there is some logic
to longitude's sleight of hand.
Like the televised magician
who before my eyes
made the Statue of Liberty
disappear. Later, in an interview,
he explained how he had done it
with smoke and light and mirrors.

I chose to believe it
anyway. The sky growing
dark around it. How it shimmered
for a moment and was gone.

Learning How to Pray

When I heard my brother
was dying   youngest
of the six of us   our
lovely boy   I who in matters
of the spirit
had been always suspect
who even as a child
snubbed Mama's mealtime ritual
began finally to
pray   and fearing
I would offend
or miss completely
the rightful target of my pleas
went knocking everywhere
the Buddha's huge
and starry churning   Shiva
Vishnu   Isis   the worn
and ragged god of Ishmael
I bowed to the Druid reverence
of trees   to water   fire
and wind   prayed to weather
to carbon   that sole link
to all things
this and other worldly
our carbon who art in heaven
prayed to rake and plow
the sweet acid stench of dung
to fly   to the fly's soiled
wing   and to the soil
I could not stop
myself   I like a nymphomaniac
the dark promiscuity
of my spirit   there
for the taking   whore
of my breaking heart   willing
to lie down   with anything.

SLEEPING WITH MY BROTHER

Like dreaming
and knowing while you dream
you dream
this one night—despite
propriety's ragged
manifesto—this one night
with your brother
in this one bed

all night
your front to his back
breasts to shoulder blades
belly pressed
to the long sweet
slide of spine
to the right-now-still-alive
miracle
of blood and bone

all night
you don't sleep
all night
beyond the lift
and fall of your arm
curved around the curve
of this one chest
you watch the lights
of the Christmas tree
their soft pulsing
like the chronic idling
beneath your palm

all night
like the back rider
of a down-hill run-away
sled you do the only
thing   you can do
close your eyes
and hold on

~~~ PERIPHERAL RESURRECTIONS ~~~

THREE

It was one of those moments you wish you could marry forever.
—James Seay

My father, as he pulled
off his beaten shoes and unbuttoned his shirt
after a hard day in the spinning
room, the whistle he would ease through the slit
between his tongue and palate, too tired
to press his lips into the tight o
of the realer whistle whistled Sunday mornings
before the world went bad, the clear,
pure strains of *Fraulein* called up
from his healing lungs

Beth's snowflakes,
before she died, how, when she opened
the door to let us in, hundreds
of them she had cut and hung from the ceiling—
sloppy paper flakes spinning above the heat
of the big-bellied stove, unbelievable
soft blizzard of white

the look on Flint's face,
its sweet incredulity of loss
as if in the telling of the story
he suddenly realized the girl
in the men's restroom of that New Orleans
oyster house was the one true love of his life,
the way he turned from the urinal
and there she was, pushing him aside
pleading—*I'm going to throw up*
and I'll need you to hold my hair—
and, done, she was gone, as he stood there
stunned, still holding his penis,
his other hand cupped tight to his mouth and nose,
breathing in, breathing deep
the still lingering jasmine of her hair.

You Can't Drive the Same Truck Twice

for my ex-husband

When I heard the sudden
thunder of my husband's truck
explode into the drive
and saw him, after ramming
the defective gear-stick
into neutral, emerge crazy-eyed
and fevered, fling up
the battered hood, go down
and disappear beneath its open wound
of primer, I knew how the evening
would go. How deep into moonlight
he would hang like Jonah, half in,
half out, his full weight given
to the wrench, gripped to the stripped
bolts and nuts, capping and uncapping
the ancient battery, his body
lost to that odd carcass of scavenged parts.
I loved him for his love of broken things—
the handleless hoes and axes, the sprung
rumble seat bought years ago
at auction, the legless chairs
retrieved from garbage heaps,
that truck each day he reinvented.
Like the rivers of Heraclitus. Like Van Gogh's
olive trees and irises that quiver,
still. Bristle. As if caught forever
in the antique instant of their opening.
It's why we love Jesus, some philosopher
once said, instead of God. Why lovers
love the moon that's always falling.

THE SCAR

The first time I saw his naked
body rising above me
from the couch where all day
I had memorized for my art history final
the rudiments of line and medium and hue
I thought Michelangelo's *David*
had stepped out of its binding,
the papery thighs and forearms
bulging to life, the shoulders,
the heavy penis ripped
from the glossy pages, the stone,
for centuries cupped and ready
in the perfected tension
of his hand, laid finally down.

We were eighteen then, and I had never seen
anything so beautiful—that body,
lifting from my own inadequate body,
the small breasts, the pale, skinny
arms and thighs that didn't deserve
his loveliness—and would have turned,
afterwards, self-consciously away
had it not been for the scar (emergency
appendectomy, I later learned). Had it not been
for the ragged stigmata of that wound,
purple phalanx of cells that must have rallied hard
for a boy of twelve, little army of flesh
gathering together for his life.

Years later after love, I would watch
him sleeping, his chest rippling
like a quilt laid to air against the windy grass,
his hair curled, graying, at his temples,
and I knew, finally, the wisdom
of old philosophers, how what is real
exists only in the realm of the unchanging.
Like that scar, lifting and falling,
that lovely, immutable banner of his breathing.

WANTED

Nights I crawled in beside him,
tired from his books, exhaustion
and poverty spooned between us

like the ménage-à-trois we once saw
in some dirty movie, and fell
into the long double-shift

of dreams, that conveyor belt, stinking
and gummy from the scantily wrapped
breasts of chicken and the mutilated

cans of soup and spaghettios, the nightly
joke of the meat department boys
or the ones who worked in stock, who

grabbed naps on giant sacks of Alpo
when business was slow. My ankles
throbbed in my sleep and the faces

of customers kept rising
out of the clang and roar
of registers. The long-married

couple who bought two supplies
of groceries, the bottom of their cart
like the Continental Divide

or those invisible boundaries
children swipe across the hot
backseats of cars. They would turn

their backs to each other, wadding
the damp, thin dollars to their hearts,
making sure the other couldn't see

into the stingy caverns of their separate
wallets. And the two who bought
their groceries one at a time,

their snowy heads appearing at my counter
ten times a day for those game cards
you could scratch and match

for prizes. They never said a word
but collected their Cornflakes
or Twinkies before pausing at the sliding

doors to scrape the silvery lining
from the card as I seethed
and shoved the next customer's apples

into the innocent hands of the bagboy
at my back. It is this I will miss
years later, after the degrees, the bills

paid off and nothing left to hold us,
finally, together. This dream
I could always count on. And Sundays,

the two of us ghosting the local
post office, memorizing the faces
of murderers and thieves. Dreaming

of the rewards they carried, their scars
and stubbled faces, the beautiful broken
noses of all those saviors.

BARK

There is evidence, scientists
say, that before dogs
were domesticated, before
we rescued them from wilderness,

they howled, growled, yelped,
and whined, but did not bark.
Evidence, they say,
that hearing human

speech—*beg   sit   stay*—they
tried to mimic it
and got the bark instead.
Lost darling, casualty of my divorce,

surest way my husband knew
to punish me (so loved I named
you Seamus, Mr. Heaney to strangers
and acquaintances) remember

the night I fetched you
from your pen, the hurricane
already moving inward from the coast,
how you mistook my cautionary

measure for some midnight jamboree,
soiree du chien in celebration
of something you couldn't quite remember
but must have done right that day.

That night you were too happy
to bark, pranced in jubilation
of your middle-of-the-night reprieve
around and around the couch

where at either end my husband
and I dozed in the ostensible safety
of our living room. We had learned
already the democracy of those storms.

Three years before, our yard
untouched, every oak and hemlock
pointing as ever upward, as we stared
at our neighbor's property

reduced to sticks and stones.
Not knowing what other storms
were gathering, you continued
your solitary parade around

the room, where at intervals
we would feel against our drowsy lips
that unschooled kiss, the sudden unabashed
joy of your wet tongue. Years later,

over drinks or in the grocery
check-out line, friends catching up
on the progress of our families, how suddenly
embarrassed and put off they become

when I pull out pictures of you
and the wag-tail ghost of your name
lopes across my tongue. Then the sob,
the yelp, the whine. Almost a bark.

PERIPHERAL RESURRECTIONS

It had been the kind of day
they sing about in country/westerns:
how the drunk, the day
his mother got out of prison
to attend the funeral of his wife,
put a pistol to his head and missed,
and I just couldn't muster much enthusiasm
when I found, that evening in my mailbox,
a letter from Jacques Cousteau
insisting I alone could save the dolphin.

But later, when you stopped by
in the truck you borrowed from a friend
after your wife had wiped you out of everything,
I couldn't help but laugh at your perfected misery,
at the way your ragged face gave in
to that late-night plate of grits and sausage.

I sat, suddenly happy, watching you, brother,
and thinking of Jacques Cousteau,
his endangered angel who will dive into the depths
and with her gentle head buffet to the surface
for that first vital breath
whatever she mistakes for her just-born—
rotted oars, broken keels and rudders,
a drowning man—
though the grateful saved never knew her
and what was saved in the end
was not what she'd meant to save at all.

ASCENSION

After the hardware salesman,
I fell in love with a man who wanted
to ascend. All moondrift and solar, washed

shore and the nimbused bones of fish, his hands
a God-knead, tendering my body's own brilliant
language of grief. *Getting my light body,*

he explained, when I spoke of his thinning
arms and legs, his frame an anorexic girl's
on top of mine, the slight waist, sinewy chest

paled to the vegetable hues
of iceberg and romaine, his face
and shoulders draped in the tofu-shroud

of his flesh. But I needed evidence
of that rumored other life, so took him in.
Grunewald's most famous Christ

stepped down from his altar
into the world again. Jesus on the
lam and me, failed atheist,

ready to be washed in the blood of
anything. I learned, finally,
what it was like all those years,

my husband under the house alone,
knocking at pipes, securing the joists
and studs, the mundanities

of this life—out of my lover's
holy precinct—relegated now to me.
Battles with the shell-shocked

landlord as the floor began to sink
and the roof continued its slow leak
through the ceiling above our bed.

One night I awoke to find him
in the flung doors of the balcony.
He had taken the gauze curtains

from their rods and draped them across
his shoulders, his arms spread against
the moon's soft rising like the wings

of some angel or bat. Next morning
he was gone, transmorphosed to that place
of peace and light he'd feared my own bereft

and unenlightened soul would never know.
Ascended, I assumed, until leaving
for work I saw beyond the back door's

freshly-painted white—now splattered
in red—the four muddy ruts of his retreads
and knew he had taken the truck instead.

FLOOD

Lugging my second load
of dirty laundry up the long hill
between my cabin and the house,

I saw approaching in the distance
a machine so sleek and gleaming
it seemed itself a prayer

against the chronic dust
and labor of my sister's farm.
In the yard I stopped to catch

my breath, hoist the burgeoning
load of muddy socks and overalls
higher on my hip as the wheels

ground to a halt and you emerged
from the driver's side, waving
your bible above the balding Ararat

of your head. You must have been
a seasoned pilgrim in this land
of the terminally lost, for you lit

right in, afraid, perhaps, I might
turn irredeemably away before you'd had
the chance to reach the daily quota

of your witness. I stood with my mouth
agape in the unstoppable testimony
of your love, your

hi hello how are you
I'm Wendell and this is my wife Lorraine
and we'll only be a minute I promise
everyone being so busy these days
and isn't it a pity all the changes
looming before us sooner than we think
the warnings aplenty we've been sent
the snakes for instance and the flood
you've heard of Noah right? You do believe
in the flood don't you   surely you do….

Shut Up, Wendell. Shut up,
I would have said had you let up
a moment. Would have said, yes,

yes, I do believe, for floods,
like certain other things, happen.
Was happening at that very moment

in my sister's laundry room, a blown
hose in the rinse cycle of my first
load and the water even as you

spoke, ascending the newly-papered
walls of her dining room and den.
When my faith has gone to flotsam.

When the closest I've lately come
to salvation is the man who followed
me one night home, who looked so much

like Jesus riding the wild surge
of my lonely thighs I let him stay a year,
I think of you, Wendell, your spate

of prophecy truer than you would ever
know, your wife keeping her safe distance
at your back, the terror in her eyes

that of a dove having been for days
aloft and still no land in sight.
And me treading the waters

of my disbelief, shifting my soiled
burden from hip to hip as at that very
moment through the faulty plumbing

of my sister's ancient Kenmore
God, as always, was moving
in his one and mysterious way.

FAT MAN IN THE SAUNA

How strange the aloneness
of that day. The deserted hotel gym
where I walked a mile in my own
shoes on a machine that numbered
the openings and closings
of my heart. Then laps in the pool,
a weightless floating of the body's
ten-thousand griefs. I had driven
for hours, after the final papers
of my divorce, and checked in
to the Renaissance Hotel, alone.
It was Christmas, everything
ashimmer in that newest Jerusalem
where anything, I hoped, might be
forgiven or healed. And there he was,
of all places, when I finished
my workout, the fattest man
I had ever seen, beardless and bald,
his white groin swaddled, half sitting,
half reclining in the cedary-sweet
warmth of the sauna, slowly eating
an apple. *Come in* he said, calmly,
quiet between bites, between
the skin's delicate breaking
and the soft ruminations
of his tongue.   *Come in* he said.

And I went in

TRAVELING IN TIME OF DANGER

TOURING THE BERLINER DOM, JANUARY, 1990

What I remember most
about the long descent
into the crypt
of the bombed cathedral
was not the tenured dust,
nor the scattered bones
of emperors, bones of their sons
and daughters, nor all the cherubs
tumbled, their terrible lips
and noses hacked away.
Nor how, as our guide explained,
they dug later in, experts
kicking light into the dark
like frenzied angels,
gone down to verify
which armbone, shin,
match the startled
clavicles and ribs.
But how, after we climbed, blinded,
back into our lives, yes,
what I remember most
was how we turned
when at the perimeter of our group
a man, aged seventy, knelt
at his old wife's feet,
slowly on one knee
and tied her shoe, looped
one string carefully
across the other
and pulled it through, tightening
the worn laces into a solid bow.
We stood there quiet and watched him
tie her shoe, pat it, then turn gently
to the still-tied other one and tighten it, too.

HAIR

Always, when one travels with students
there is the problem of hair,
more urgent than the Croats and Serbs,
than the repatriated Haitian
screaming *I'd rather be dead*
as he slipped the saving rope they'd tossed him
around his throat, then, flailing the waves
like the Neanderthal breast of God,
went madly under.

Again and again you explain
in your most serious teacher-voice
the practicality of converters, rudiments
of volt and charge, but they know
all voltage is the same, nudge each other
and wink, the way relatives
talk their secret talk
in the bedrooms of the dying.

So, later in the privacy of their rooms
they plug into this foreign world
that to their surprise sputters
and fizzles then glows a brighter
bright before the lights shut down,
before the entire floor
goes black as East Berlin
and the little concierge
comes stamping, pounding
the derelict air above his balding head.

You smile, reader. You smile, knowing
as well as I the importance of being coiffed,
of hair washed and blown just so
for that long journey up the Zugspitz
or, say, the drive to Dachau
where we all want to look our best
in case we see ourselves reflected
in the ovens' dull glaze, still heavy
with the memory of flesh the villagers
swore they never smelled. Or if they did,
thought it only their daughters
dressing for their handsome evening soldiers,
too dreamy to realize
they'd held the glowing rod
too long inside those delicate
human curls.

THE ENTRY

In Paris there is a hospital
and a police station, I read
from the yellow pages of my journal,
though I had forgotten, or pushed
somehow from memory, that one pathetic entry
scrawled on our seventh day
in the most beautiful city in the world.
But there they are, years later,
those words streaked like snuff
across the page, a stagnant pond
through which her face now rises,
that bright senior dreaming of graduation,
her future almost close enough to kiss.
And there, too, the face she later recalled,
as she wept, tugging at the inadequate gown
the nurse insisted she put on. Face
of that young man who spoke no English
in his pointed snakeskin shoes
and leather jacket, dark eyes
and bushy brows that spun her pulsing
amid the colored lights of the discothèque
and then, the white interior of his car,
the room he dragged her screaming to,
strewn with women's lingerie and shoes.
And afterwards, the odd distant keen
of sirens, all night, as she lay there
still beside him, staring into the dark,
into the rest of her only life.

Traveling in Time of Danger

Outside the Gellert Hotel
the sun comes up as usual
above the Danube that keeps on going
between the sprawled, lovely banks
of Buda and Pest, despite
the pre-dawn news the airwave static
delivered to our rooms: Iraq
bombed, and little Kuwait,
as promised, now avenged.
Our families want us home.
One student begins her frantic packing
though I keep assuring her,
ironic as it may seem, that the safest
time to travel is in time of danger.
And truly, after a hijacking
or the invasion of some small place
too insignificant to note, airports
and railways burgeon with guards,
so many it seems there's one for each of us,
our own personal saviors, machine guns
slung across their breasts
like children being carried to safety.
But by now she's finished—her baggage
stuffed with tiny dolls
stiff in the obsolete clothing
of their histories—and has called a cab
to take her to the airport where she'll wait,
counting her breaths, trusting the troops
already gathering, flooding
the gates and runways. Like the rivers
of that country she'll go home to,
the rivers that must have run there
in the first days of its life,
the first good days of its life.

In Salzburg, Austria, a Student Learns His Father Is Dead

"But they were estranged,"
the students keep explaining
when I express surprise
at his decision not to go back home.
He snaps too quickly back
into the easy banter of co-eds,
laughs too loud and often
for a boy who's lost his father,
as I lost mine, twice
in this same life.
Today he'll go together
with us down
into the mines they named
the city for. Four hundred feet
below the white world
where we'll board the little ferry,
our guide a leder-hosened
Charon, laughing hard
at our bad German, at all
our exclamations
of terror and delight.
And salt! Salt crusted
everywhere! We'll touch
the hazel rock gleaming
above our heads, bring
our fingers to our tongues,
tasting the briny core, deeper
than we dreamed
we would ever have to go.

FOR THE BODY

St. Patty's Day and hordes
of would-be Irish filled the streets,
decked in their greens and high on Guiness

and blarney and everyone in love and me, too,
though I had sunk for just a moment to the curb,
dizzy from the strains of *Danny Boy*

some tattooed drunk kept wailing
in my ear. So there I was, eye-level
with that torrent of knees poking from holey

jeans, the worn and dusty boots of bikers
who'd thundered for the morning into town,
goose-bumpy thighs of teeny-boppers

rushing the season in their mini-skirts
and shorts. And I was thinking,
as I'm prone to do when I'm drunk and feeling

philosophic, about Descartes, night
after night in his little study
burning all those candles, as if

it really mattered which, the body
or the mind, is easier to know. It was then
I saw her, that skeleton of a girl, or saw,

at least, the part of her that propelled
her through the crowd, those sticks of legs,
like something dead amidst the burgeoning

mass of shins and ankles. I started to reach
for her, as if without my help she would crumple,
small mound of twig and straw before my eyes.

How she must have hated that trapping
of flesh, that albatross, jail-cell
of the spirit she would gladly be rid of.

And, yet, there it was, all over her arms
and face, that delicate growth of hair,
that halo of warmth her body in desperation

had spun, like the blown silk of milkweed,
like the bleached coat of some animal
grown long ago extinct, pale fur

the flesh in unrequited love had wrapped
her in. Then she was gone, borne
by that wave of strangers, and I, sobering,

went back to my green beer, to Descartes,
brooding above his silvery river of wax,
the exhausted wick going finally down, and out.

From Rome

Evenings I go down to the Spanish Steps
beneath the window where Keats died,
take my place among the derelicts
and lovers, and write to my family

in the mill town where I grew up. I shuffle
through postcards—Bernini's and Donatello's,
various sun-lit angles of the Coliseum,
home to the homeless cats treading

the ancient stone, the atavistic
taste of Christian still lingering
on their tongues, to the one I bought
for my uncle, the one I'm sure he's seen

in picture books, God touching
Adam to life amid the pagan sybils
and ignudi of the Sistine Ceiling.
I love knowing how he will brighten

to find something in his mail,
odd word from the world
he slipped long ago out of, though
each Thursday he appears

at my mother's door, bearing
his gift of love—two wild cherry
cough drops glistening like jewels
in the extended craziness of his hand.

He touches the tip of his old cap
and he's off again, shadowboxing
his way back home and up the long stairs
to his third floor room where he will

tape to his window this card,
its bright colors facing into the street,
as if the strangers who pass each day below
could see, if they glanced up, this Dionysian

Adam, propped on his elbow, lifting
in non-chalance his powerful finger.
And God, his hair and beard
blowing furiously in the painted wind,

the curious horde at his back, and Eve
wedged in the circle of his arm, her frail
lovely shoulders pulling away,
not much wanting that world

she alone can see waiting there
in the small hard space
between their fingertips.

Slow

I like the joke about the snail
who mugged the turtle
who when asked by the policeman
to recount the sequence of events
couldn't *because it all happened so fast.*

It's the only joke I know,
the one I always preface—*Stop me
if you've heard it*—though friends
who love me crack up each time, slap
each other on the back,
and laugh themselves to tears.

I want a life that slow.
Like George, the idiot savant,
who couldn't spell his name
or count to ten, but could remember
for the talk-show host, the weather
of any day she named—her high school
graduation, Pearl Harbor,
the day the Rosenbergs were killed.

I'll tell you the truth, he would begin,
the year washing slowly back, cresting,
sweet wave against his tongue,
the little ark of months and days
come to rest on Ararat. *June 7, 1959.*
Warm and sunny that one was, and then,
the wreck of his old hand rising toward the sky,
The truth I've told will get me into heaven.

I want a life that slow. To lumber
each morning out of the slush
and mire, my earthly possessions

strapped across my spine. And like
George, famous for making small-talk,
I'll turn to you, good friend, idling
on the stump next door, the wound-down
clock of your body glistening in the light,

And *Stop me if you've heard this*, I'll begin
as your eyes bank with tears, happy
with this old joke, this weather,
this truth I've told, again.

A BOOK OF MINUTES

For Paul Baker Newman
mentor and friend
1919–2004

I who believe in prayer but could never in God
place roses at your grave with nothing to divine of snow.

—Agha Shahid Ali

And for these living:
Jerry Stockdale, Richard Goode,
Billy Wireman, and Bob Haden

Do I dare
Disturb the universe?
In a minute there is time
For decisions and revisions which a minute will reverse.

   —T.S. Eliot
    from "The Love Song of J. Alfred Prufock"

~~~ MATINS ~~~

Rosemary

Prostratus, Alba, Severn Sea
good memory
you bequeath. And
to the woman

who wears you on her head, a man
who will be true.
It has been said
when Mary on

her flight to Egypt laid her cloak
on you, your stunned
white blossoms turned
suddenly blue.

Yarrow

Oh, bitter sweet Achillea,
the men you must
have saved to earn
his name, he who

knew how well your feathered leaves
staunch the flow of
blood. How we must
defame you! Who

use you now for acne's surest
cure, the quick
decomposi-
tion of manure.

HOREHOUND

Seed of Horus, Eye of the Star,
Bull's blood. Oh where
did Granddaddy
get the stuff! Treats

bitter as quinine he reached for,
yes, whenever
we visited.
Still, beneath that

gall was just enough sweet to lure
us back for more.
Odd, still, how much
we miss the stuff.

SORREL

to my father

Blackfoot woman you would never
know, what made her
name you that? Name
you kept hidden

from your friends who answered to Bill
or Joe. Silly.
Unmanly you
said. You who knew

only stories. How the mare she
had loved broke the
fence when she died.
How hard you cried.

CHAMOMILE

Maythen to the Anglo-Saxon.
Egypt's minion
offered up to
sun. Little weed

of our childhood picked to appease
our mother's ire
when father turned
to drink. Too soon

we learn, as field and cove and ditch
we tread, the more
it is trodden
the more it spreads.

THYME

Before magic's sad demise, your
leaves could conjure
fairies, render
gallant in war

a lady's knight-errant. And no
sweeter praise of
her might he tell
than that she smelled

of you. Once you were said to cure
shyness and fear
when quaffed with a
dram of good beer.

Then you went looking for other
work. Dabbled for
a while in teas
and stews, posies

and light cosmetics, finally
straggling back to
your first employ,
embalmer of

the freshly dead. Even now, we
can almost hear
the faint, sure hum
of your tenure.

~~~ LAUDS ~~~

To St. Wilgefortis,
Protectress of Virgins and Unhappy Wives

You'd think the name itself would have
frightened him off.
Rendered null that
prayer you sent

up to God to maim or blemish
you. How stunned your
pagan suitor
must have been, how

overcome with tears, to behold
upon your once
exquisite face
a full grown beard.

TO ST. CHRISTINA THE ASTONISHING, PROTECTRESS OF LUNATICS

Many swore by your piety.
Adored you for
the way you rolled
yourself in flames

and leapt into freezing waters.
Praised you even
more when you soared
from your casket

to the beams where for days you squawked
and screamed. Others,
though, were mixed in
their opinions.

To St. Fiacre,
Patron of the Lowliest

Little friend of the nether parts,
curer of warts
and fistulas,
of syphilis

and worms. So grateful to you are
we, the Figs of
Saint Fiacre
we have christened

our hemorrhoids. Forgive us, though,
if seldom we
bestow your name
upon our boys.

To St. Lucy of Syracuse, Protectress of Writers

Dearest Lucy, you knew our plight.
When you refused
to prostitute
yourself, they tore

out your eyes. Then they tried to burn
you at the stake,
but the flames like
firey birds just

flew away. Finally, they thrust
a dagger in
your throat, and that
was all she wrote.

To St. Brendan the Navigator, Protector of Sailors

Who among us has not tossed for
years, bereft, your
kind, adrift in
the foamy brine,

searching for some strange and perfect
world where we might
begin anew,
unaware there

is always a veil that hides the
paradise we
seek, that always
we are the veil.

To Saint Vitus,
Patron of Comedians

Side-kick to the slap and the stick,
sure as any
god to salvage
us, will you be

the one we summon in the end?
Wanting nothing
of the rained and
rubbling world save

one final chicken ambling now
across the high.
Someone hell-bent
on knowing why.

~~~ PRIME ~~~

HURRICANE ECONOMICS

Seven days the power out. One
merchant gave his
ice away, doled
out the dwindling

blocks and bags like the potatoes
and butter and
beans of Hoover
Days. When there was

no more, his competitor down
the street doubled
the price, made a
killing from ice.

Elegy for Enkidu

You'd never have left on your own.
You so at home
with beast and fowl.
Gods are cruel,

though, knowing few men can resist
a woman's breasts.
Knowing how when
you turned again

toward wilderness, deer and leopard,
too, from you would
flee. A story
old as the sea.

WHEN BETH DIED

for Becky McClanahan

No cards, no casseroles. Just you
at my closed door
offering to
do my nails. How

tenderly you worked, as if in
fear my fingers
too might break. Clipped,
trimmed, and polished

until each was a perfect arc,
tiny gleaming
bridge waiting for
someone to cross.

MY GRANDMOTHER'S NEW PIANO

Her coal-singed hands drew music like
a poultice from
its keys where in
her weathered house

all else looked-shabby now. *Yours when
I'm gone*, she said.
I like to think,
in that one month

before the collectors came, her
fingers had to
ask permission
for them to rest.

My Mother's Lexicon

You were the first poet, Mama.
The language of
others never
vociferous

enough. Dad didn't *patronize*
old man Causey's
bar, he *stayed laid
up down there*. Paid

not with cash but *rags from his younguns'
backs*. Not once did
he *come home,*
he *straggled in.*

WHEN MY FATHER ASKED ME TO WASH HIS BACK

He stood there at the kitchen sink
(late fall, I think)
shirtless and hung
over, his lungs

long gone to brown from double shifts.
His hands shook, gripped
the rusty rim
as I swiped a

single S across his back and
fled. Nights, still, I
lie in fear there
really is a

hell.

For My Friend's Mother, Dead at 94

Lengthwise instead of cross you sliced.
How like sacred
fish you dredged the
pieces, slithered

each with care into the sizzling
black pan. Tiny
Agnes, I would
tell you now, as

they lift away your glasses and
close the lid, I'll
never fry squash
the same again.

FOR JIMMIE M.

Even for the time you yelled at
me, balled up your
fist and banged it
on the sideboard

when I told you I was leaving
my husband. Yours
had died twenty
long years before.

You were on a trip. Got the news
by telephone.
Now you, yours, and
mine—air dirt stone.

~~~ TERCE ~~~

How I Became an Existentialist

The year I got no Valentines,
it was snowing
deep outside. I'd
probably walked

five miles on cardboard soles. The boy
behind me must
have seen, tried hard
to muffle the

sound as he ripped his own big heart
in two. The part
he handed me
said only, *Be.*

MYSTERY OF THE SPHINX

"Marsh," Gabe would softly say and nod
toward the Red
Baron lazing
by a sunny

window sill. She'd turn from her book
to take a look,
then both begin
to chuckle in

sheer delight. I'd look up, too, but
all I saw? Fat
cat on a chair
just lying there.

GIVE UNCLE WARDY A BIG KISS, MAMA SAID

His face a roiling caldron
of cysts and wens,
we cringed at just
the thought of it.

But when he knelt to pull us close
oh what a host
of gum and mints
came tumbling out!

How were we to know someone that
furuncular
could prove so quite
avuncular?

FOR MY DOG, WHO LISTENS TO ALL MY POEMS

How entranced, each time, she sits there,
her eyes, I swear,
filling with tears
at her master's

inimitable brilliance. It's
clear to me what's
bounding through her
head: *The greatest,*

yet, of all the generations!
My husband says
she's just waiting
for her rations.

False Spring

On a day too beautiful to
be dutiful,
I'm tempted to
call in sick. But

sun alone has fevered up this
brow, my only
cough a chough, wing-
ing above my

house. Why can't that frog beyond the moat
be in my throat?
Oh, what the hell,
I'll call in well.

I Ask Forgiveness of My Feet

Summers, too, I banished you. Skewed
you into shoes
sizes smaller
than my younger

sister wore. Odd simian toes,
poor bunions grown
in self-defense
of such senseless

arrogance. I am older now
and wise. I would
take you, even
bare, anywhere.

~~~ SEXT ~~~

Anatomy of a Southern Kiss

She said, *Just put your stuff right there.*
He said, *Right whar?*
Mimicking her
Carolina

drawl. Tells now how it took so long,
that dreaded *No,*
(Oh, man's worst curse)
oozing from her

lovely mouth, he'd tasted each slow
sweet *0, 0, 0*
before she could
get the word out.

By the Time We Get to Athens, I'm Going to Look Like a Greek God, He Said.

But squats and barbells hurt his back.
He then tried track
that soon became
too crowded. Some

nut kept hogging his jogging space.
Through snow and ice
and into spring
the only thing

that stiffened was his upper lip
when he asked if
I'd settle for
a messenger.

At a Topless Beach on Mykonos I Make a Deal with Jerry

You'll like it, he keeps insisting,
meaning baring
my breasts like all
the ballsy rest

courting the bright Aegean. Three
Ouzos later
and I'm halter
free as he pens

his prudish mother: *Cathy looks*
just marvelous
tanned and topless.
Wish you were here.

ON INISHMORE

All day the village children had
been gathering
sticks. Debris to
feed the flames of

St. John's Eve. Next morning you would
be boating in
to marry me
on that lovely

bleak island where I had gone to
teach. Each hour
seemed the wraith of
that stubborn old

saint, time having somehow betrayed
its long ago
promise to pass.
When at last I

knew, love, sleep that night would never
come for me, I
rose and dressed and
climbed to the bluff

alone to watch and wait. All night
I waited and
I watched the long
slow fires burn.

In Praise of Bald Men

Glory be to God for shiny
things. Sweet orbs. Sweet
sublunary
spheres devoid of

mundane hair. Come, my brilliant one,
trust me now whose
hungry fingers
navigate what

luminates each night our astral
bed. Whose tongue must
needs explore such
heavenly head.

Evening Primrose

Statutory flower, I tease
my husband as
he leans in close
and softly blows

into a still half-open bud.
*Be patient, would
you,* I whisper
as she quivers

to full blossom beneath his breath.
He turns to me
and smiles. A warm
breeze lifts my dress.

~~~ NONE ~~~

THE EYE

Even in ancient Egypt, the
word *Maa* meant *to*
see. Sweet honor
too soon turned curse.

Medusa's daughter. Lady of
slaughter. "See you
later," Father
would mutter as

he left for a night of lust. And
under Ma's breath
always, "Not if
I see you first."

THE SKIN

Why are you smiling? You died weeks
 ago. All, at
 least, that can be
 seen of you. Coat

of many colors, you were soul's
first clothing. Chain
mail against a
warring world. You

are sloughing as we speak. Sweet lips,
forehead, chin, and
blushing cheek. Dust
beneath our feet.

JOINT AND BONE

Sweet temperomandibular,
odd song of our
creaking jaws, you
gambol off the

doctor's tongue like a game of chance.
Oh, beautiful
epiphesus,
in the final

dare, one thing's for sure. We'll go first.
You next, and all
your comely names.
And then our own.

THE KIDNEYS

We can thrive on one alone, though
blessed with two. So
generous a
little member

of the body's relentless crew.
Here's half for you,
they seem to say,
like twins taught good

manners at an early age. They
could be beans. Wings
in air. Hands about
to close in prayer.

The Heart

Even in the womb it seems not
to know what it
is, swimming first
in its small sea

like the heart of a fish. Then, as
if having dreamt
of air, feigning
heart of frog and

then of snake. Soon it has no choice
but to claim its
own. Four-chambered.
Clenched. Size of a

fist.

The Duodenum

Turnstile, tollbooth, ferryman. Means
but not an end.
Without you we're
doomed, yet where is

the bard who ever sang of you?
No Tell-Tale Du-
odenum or
of Darkness. How

still you wait in the body's deep
wood. Was ever
there a Hunter
lonely as you?

Harvest Time

Six hours at most, the heart. To lift
it up and lay
it down again.
Not so, the liver.

Tireless little Baptist, it will
tread for us
morning until
dusk this river

of air. But the kidneys, oh! Three
whole days since the
spirit passed, and
Christ! with us still.

 VESPERS

FLYING TO SAUSALITO WITH MY SISTERS

In a cloud above the Badlands
Rosie's right hand
newly bandaged.
Beside her, rage

disguised—tiny carcinoma
grazing Trisha's
wrist. Under my
arm the knot I've

just discovered. Our bodies' deep
cargo of grief
enroute to our
dying brother.

LABOR DAY

Morning's IV done, all his pills,
he turns to Bill's
gift of Melon—
icy sweet chunks

of honeydew brought home from the
local deli.
I watch each bite
he takes then wipe

his chin. *Unbelievable*, he
says and lifts a
bite to me. Says,
here, just taste this.

RELATIVE

At intervals I leave the news
of Diana's
death to adjust
my still brother's

IV. I touch his damp forehead,
smooth his blanket,
count each rising,
each sure falling

of his chest, then return to her
crushed Mercedes,
the crowds, my good
and shameful luck.

THE ARBORIST EXPLAINS THE SITUATION

How cheap do you want it? he asks,
trying to mask
his anger, Bill's
counter offer still

way too far below the going
fee. *A dead tree
can be trouble.*
He's got double

that price before. *Six months at most.
You'll have no
choice when those
limbs begin to fall.*

When My Mother Speaks of Loneliness

I offer to bring her some books,
the new Updike,
an Oscar Wilde
she hasn't read.

My brother is dead, her youngest,
his ashes just
settled in their
urn. *No,* she turns

to me and says, *bring* Shane,
The Grapes of Wrath ... *bring* Rain.
The ones I've read
before and loved.

THE TRUNK

I envied my dog that option—
the rattan trunk
chewed this morning
to twig. All night

I had warded off that dream, my
brother alive
once more, asking
if I'd like to

see the trick again. All night, this.
And beyond the
wall, the gnashing
of my dog's teeth.

TORGE

Three years after your death, when I
can smile once more,
I recall the
story you loved

to tell, about asking your grade
school teacher to
spell *torge* for you.
Torge? she asked in

sheer bewilderment. *Torge*, you said
again. *Like "The
prince rode torge the
castle on a*

big white horse."

Watching Bill's New Lover Prepare Our Evening Meal

Not much, really, has changed. The San
Anselmo sun
streams still into
the room so bright

it almost blinds. And, yes, here still,
the vast array
of kitchen tools
that loved your hands.

See how they glisten now in his.
Dexterous and
able. Almost
as beautiful.

 COMPLINE

PANSY

So I've come to love the flower
whose name some jerk
shouted at my
brother as we

walked past. Beneath my dormant rose,
it alone bears
the weight of snow.
Pensées. Thoughts no

less numerous than its many
names: *Call me to
you. Hearts-ease. Kiss
me ere I rise.*

Driving Through the Mountains, I Remember How My Friend Was Brought to Tears

when he spoke of all the apples
fallen along
the road, the cars
that kept right on

going. It seemed all the old wounds
of his past would
open then. Such
goodness left on

the ground to rot—oh, wild, red hearts
offering their
sweet essence to
the tongueless air.

To the Oldest Live Oak in the South

Even in winter, green. It's why
we call you *live*.
That or the way
gray mosses stay,

amidst your leaves, their own demise.
What human cries,
old man, have you
been witness to?

You're not talking, though. Just silence
and through your dense
knotted limbs, a
revenant wind.

FOR OKRA

I'd never seen so green a green
before, so lean
those tender pods
I stopped and bought

when I knew for certain you were
not on that plane.
Trish, what would my
selfish life have

been? But no—come get some okra
now. I've dredged and
fried it. Just the
way you like it.

CREPE MYRTLES

When the heaviness of dog days
has had its way
with us, they bloom
to stay the doom

of summer's end. Such popsicles,
these crepe myrtles,
to cool the day's
parched tongue! And where's

the truck that brought them? The little
bell? Clang goes the
ghostly driver
and then is gone.

DIGITALIS

Legend says bad fairies taught sly
fox to wear you
on his toes to
mute among the

hens his dreaded steps. Is this why,
then, when Mother
began to die
it was you the

doctors filled her with, quieting
for awhile the
relentless paw-
ing at her door?

APPROPRIATE CONTAINER

She thought it was time I found one.
Three years and then
some, my brother's
ashes, swaddled

in the green velvet bag a friend
had once given
me wine in. A
month later I

did. Satin lined. Shrouded in spring
flowers. Safe in
the soft crook of
her folded arm.

Peace Lilies

I collect them now, it seems. Like
sea-shells or old
thimbles. One for
Father. One for

Mother. Two for my sweet brothers.
Odd how little
they require of
me. Unlike the

ones they were sent in memory
of. No sudden
shrilling of the
phone. No harried

midnight flights. Only a little
water now and
then. Scant food and
light. See how I've

brought them all together here in
this shaded space
beyond the stairs.
Even when they

thirst, they summon me with nothing
more than a soft,
indifferent furl-
ling of their leaves.

THE CANDLE I HOLD UP
TO SEE YOU

DEDICATION

I dedicate this book to all my earthly angels who held me in the world when I did not want to be here.

First, to my brother-in-law Clyde E. Buchanan, empirical evidence that God in one of his many incarnations drives a red truck. To my beloved and steadfast sisters and brothers—Patricia Smith Buchanan, Rosemary Smith Tipton, and Allen Dale Smith. To my brother-in-law J.R. Tipton and sister-in-law Julie Davis Smith. To Carli Rose Buchanan and her creators, Noel and Brandi. To Heather Tipton. To Anna and Andy. To Jerry Rhodus. To Aunt Juanita.

To my cherished son and daughter—Jeff Stockdale and Jenny Stockdale.

To the real POETS in my life—Marsha Purvis, Charlotte Shaw, Lou Hayes, Debby Hegler, and Jim Mullis (posthumously).

To Gabe Purvis.

To my sisters in poetry—Eleanor Brawley, Ione O'Hara, Dede Wilson, Diana Pinckney, and Mary Martin. To Terri Wolfe and Louise Rockwell.

To my homey, my Fire, my partner in literary crime—Karon Gleaton Luddy.

To the faculty, staff, and students of The Haden Institute, especially Bob and Mary Ann Haden, Diana McKendree, Joyce Rockwood Hudson, Susan Sims Smith, Layne Rasche, and Chelsea Wakefield. To Joann Hassler, Rita Travis, and Karen Blaha.

To the faculty, staff, and students of Queens University of Charlotte, especially those in the low-residency MFA Program. Liz Strout, I love you bunches.

To Pam Hildebran.

To my great Smokies' loves.

To John Lane and Betsy Teeter.

To the town of Tryon, North Carolina, especially Tommy and Missy Lytle, Jay and Betsy Goree, Candy Butler, Sue Campbell, Sandy McCormack, Frances Smith, Dan and Angelica Ferebee (posthumously), Pat and Ike Wilson, Monica Jones and Terry Ackerman, and Jeff and Helen Byrd. And to all the guys at Trade Street Gallery Coffee House.

A special thanks—more than I could every express—to Bob, Carmen and Beto Cumming.

~~~ EIGHT NAMES FOR GOD ~~~

וְהוּ

This, the Kabbalah tells us,
is the first name of God.
With us from the beginning
in the darkened houses
of our beings, the switch
that was always there
waiting only
to be turned on.

The name that loves us so,
it will suffer us, unkind,
to go back in time, undo
before they do to us
our ancient crimes.

Cain's bruised and battered
fist once more unscathed.
Booth's yet unfired revolver
nestled in his vest.
Lizzie's axe returned
unbloodied to its shed.

Just rest your eyes, the book
instructs, on the untranslatable
beauty of each character.
Now look!

There's Abel well among his flock again.
The Bordens bent content to their daily tasks.
And Abe, old Abe, in the high safe chamber
of his balcony—applauding—still.

Heavenly hurt, Miss Emily
called it, *imperial affliction*
sent us of the air. We've

all been there. Yet here
is the name that says we can
reclaim those sparks that once

emblazoned us. Like the stars
we walk beneath each night,
their own light dead for eons

we are told. Though there they are
above the browning ash and oak
strung high before our eyes

in the wintry limbs. Little
Promethei of our dampered souls,
go forth, go forth, and high—

plunder for us now
those still bright realms
of sky.

סִיט

Not miracle, but metaphor,
the pundits now say,
citing the bright machinations

of myth, a logical explanation
for everything—Moses' parted sea,
Joshua's stopped sun, Goliath

on his knees at David's feet.
Who could dare deny this name
evoked for conjuring such?

Listen: In the village of Medjugorge
above the craggy slopes of Apparition
Hill, the sun does more than shine—

it dances, spins, and bleeds
as Mary, 5:40 on the dot each day,
reveals herself to a cadre

of peasant youths in the loft
of old St. James. Their tender
lips move silent and young heads

nod, as if in sure agreement
with someone not quite there.
Onlookers look and flockers flock,

the faithful click of their cameras
amazing the darkening
air.

עֹלֶם

If the brain is merely
a radio, receptor
of the twin broadcasts
of Light and Dark, then
my mother kept hers tuned
both day and night
to the non-stop static airwaves
of Station HELL.

If ninety-nine things
were immaculate with her brood
she would pluck at that single
imperfection, the way
her own mother plucked
at the feathers of chickens
doomed for the old black pot.

She died swearing
the nurses, vigilant at her bed,
were *throwing off* on her—
her phrase for making fun,
demeaning, putting cruelly down.

Had she only known this name
evoked for ridding heart and mind
of bleak imaginings, she might
have been more like me.
The perfect girl she wanted
all along. Not at all obsessed
with despairing thoughts—
at least none of my own.
Just those of hers, after all
these years, I can't stop
dwelling on.

מַהֵשׁ

So this is the name
I might have called upon
when I needed
of my latest childhood ailment
to be healed. But who

in her right mind
would have chosen
in those days
to be rendered well?
The way my mother

pampered me, yes, loved
me more than all the rest
when I was ill. All day
her smooth hand grazed
my fevered brow, the clean

warm cloth tucked soft
between the poultice
she had rubbed into my chest
and the flannel gown
I'd lounged inside

for days. Finally
just the two of us—
the others packed off
to school, my father
to the mill to pull

his double shift. And always
my mother's ironing board
erected close to my
couch-turned-into-bed.
Steam rose like angels

from my father's khaki
shirts as the days
of other people's lives
flickered their bright
promise across the black

and white. *My stories,*
she called them, the only thing,
she claimed, that kept her
sane. She didn't know
the word *sane* meant *health.*

Neither did I until years
later, French 101, when
the teacher demonstrated
for us all a proper Parisian
toast. *A votre sane,* she spoke

in her most elegant dialect,
then raised a ghostly vessel
to the class. *To your health,*
in any language, this name
of God proclaims.

The only name I know
to call upon, now
that she is gone.

Like receiving a letter from God
and not bothering to open it,
a friend once replied, when I spoke

of the nightly congregation of dreams
I tended to ignore. Kabbalah, too, affirms
our dreams yet another name for God,

name that journeys us each night
to the place where water runs uphill
and people fly. Each a divine gratuity.

Counselor or little priest. Doctor attending
patient to our ills. But what of the night
you peered into that mirror to find your eye

no longer just an eye, but a bright bright
bright aquarium. How the seaweed ribboned,
bannering upwards toward the water's

silvery surface and the little fish that swam
in their rosy stippled skins, bubbling air like
rainbowed baubles from their gills. Back and

forth, forth and back they went and you loved
them and missed them when you woke, ran
to the mirror dismayed to find your eye

only an eye again—iris of palest blue,
cornea lashed with ordinary lash,
dark pupil a small stopped sun devoid

of any light. Yet years later, when doubt
shadows like a pall, remorse and guilt
and shame for all you might have been,

you conjure again that night, wrap yourself
in the realm of dream where your eye, if only
for a moment, was more—oh so much

more—than just a human eye.

אבא

After the towers
       have tumbled,
           after the day's
      good weaving
undone   undone   undone
          the little Pompeii's
   of our daily lives
reduced to shard and ash
     this is the name
         that will right
it all again

the villagers rising startled
to their dusty feet
as if from an ancient sleep.

And see how the frayed
threads gather, mend their
tattered way into the warp
and weft of some long-ago
promised shroud.

Yes, this is the name
that will raise again the beams,
conjure the girders' strength,
render whole the shattered window
panes, calling back into essence
the bright fragmented brilliance
of our lost selves.

כֵּהָת

We dreaded passing,
those Halloweens,
Ora Snipes's house,
that ramshackle porch
she held vigil on, feet
propped against the peeling
rail, chair teetering
on its hind legs
just far enough
not to let her fall, the gun
we'd heard rumor of
resting in her lap
like a child she loved,
just waiting for those of us
she didn't to step one scrawny
foot beyond the boundary
of her drive. We'd seen her

from another distance, watching
beyond the school yard's chain-link
fence, her hair a tattered web
of gray, old face the glaciered plain
that stared back each day
from the worn front covers
of our science books. We dreaded

and could not stop ourselves
from passing there, could feel,
the closer we approached, the air
around us change, as if some unseen
weight secured her guarded
house of emptiness. Had we held

in our small lexicons this name
of God, we could have stepped
there anyway—sure and light—
feeling the leaden air
dissolve, revealing the gun
for what it really was—nothing
more than a ready cache
of apples, lollipops, and gum.

~~~~ A SENTIMENTAL EDUCATION ~~~~

LANGUAGE: A SENTIMENTAL EDUCATION

How it makes and breaks you.
That tenuous stringing together
of letters and sounds. *Mean* and *amen.*
Casual and *casualty.*
Good and *god* and *dog.*

How it can turn on you.

The way my first grade teacher's eyes
bulged in disbelief
the day I ran crying to her,
tattling on the snot-nose boy
who had poked me
in my boll-weevil
with his pencil.

I can feel the mortification
of that moment still,
the class tumbling
into hysterics,
collapsing
among the jacks
and pick-up sticks
as I lifted my shirt for her to see,
the whorls of my primordial wound
reddening where his eraser had gone.

"It's time," my mother said
as I recounted, later, the sequence
of events. *Time,* she said, and began
the inevitable cleansing,
slow evacuation
of the beautiful rhetoric

of metaphor she had six years
blessed me with.
That day she gave me *navel.*
The next, *vagina* and *urinate.*
Words that could take me anywhere.

Help me, she assured,
disappear into any crowd.

Good dog.

ABATTOIR

The first time I heard the word
I imagined some faraway room
too lavish and exotic for the likes
of me. Mounds of velvet pillows,
beds carved and fluffed and canopied,

fringed shades to ease the blinding
noonday sun. In seventh grade
I was taught to get to the root of things,
all the *oirs* of our daily lives waiting
to be deciphered—*boudoir, armoire,*

reservoir—places where things of value
might safely be kept. Chambers for dreaming
ladies. Wardrobes lush with dresses, hats,
and gowns. Walled pools of clean, fresh
water to quench the browning crops.

But when that lost and lovely word
came floating back to me, I was shocked
to learn there was also a place for misery
and pain. For the once bright creatures

prodded down the line, wide-eyed,
mewling, blinking still, though the slashed
carotid, the quick, sure current of the stunning
rod had promised otherwise. How beautiful

it had sounded to me then. *Abattoir…*
Abattoir…Abattoir…. A place,
had I been invited, I might

have stepped lightly in.

WHERE'S MY FROG?

We worshipped her, Mrs. King,
who was ours for only half the day
that year. Sixth grade, our sights

on junior high and all those kids
from the good side of the tracks
she gave her mornings to

before driving to our dingy
neighborhood for history
and language arts. We

would have done anything
for her, as if having only half
rendered her more valuable,

the way we cherished our always
absent fathers, our mothers dull
in their faded aprons and always

tired, the most wretched
of commodities, being wholly
ours. One day she motioned me

to her desk, Lavon Deese, too,
a girl from up the street who'd
failed two grades, anathema

to all the other teachers whose
lessons she'd slumbered through.
The class was reading to themselves,

heads bent quiet above the hard
and colored history of our state.
We trembled on our way, the wood

beneath our soles creaking with every
step that delivered us to the vase
she'd lifted from her desk, huge globe

filled fresh each Monday with peonies
and mums, blossoms of magnolia
that rotted through the week

as the tests and essays grew,
an ominous Mt. Sinai next to them.
We couldn't believe she'd chosen us,

to deliver safely down the hall into
the girls' rest room that vase like
the holy-grail we'd learned about

at Saturday matinee, the sole purpose
of our common life now realized. In
the restroom the sun poured through

like the light in the painting my mother
had got with green stamps, Jesus offering
up his thorn-encrusted heart, the eyes

you could not escape no matter where
you sat. Into the rusty can we flung
the browning petals, their stems now limp,

leaves curled and brittling like the husks
of cicadas that signaled summer's end, then
into the nearest stall to flush beyond oblivion

the swampy dregs. When we eased into her
hands the empty vase, scrubbed and polished
to an astral sheen, our one breath stopped,

hungry for the smallest wafer of her
gratitude, stunned at what we got instead—
the slitted eye, stuck frown of her face

peering deep inside, those three bleak
words: *Where's my frog?* Our knees went
soft, the folds of our single brain calling back

the mysterious ker-plunk we'd heard
at the bottom of the commode
just as I pressed the lever.

The rest of that whole year we suffered
her disdain, we who had killed
her beloved pet, the one she brought

with her each Monday to bask
in the still primordial waters
of that week's blooms. Dark Lethe

my dreams would conjure, childhood's
defining act I would bear into the purgatory
of junior high Lavon decided to forego,

then high-school and on to college,
to the man I would finally marry,
who years later beneath the whirring

fan of an antique shop, would lift from its shelf
a small glass orb, the likes of which I'd never seen,
its surface a conglomeration of tiny holes,

and *Look*, he would say, as he handed it to
me...*a frog. I haven't seen one in years.*

I don't know what happened to Lavon.

SYNTAX

*Where haunts the ghost after the house
is gone?* I once wrote. First line of my first
poem in my first creative writing class. I'd
been reading Byron, Keats, and Shelly, lots
of Poe, loved how the cadence of their words
fit the morass my life had fallen to. I had
stayed up all night, counting stressed
and unstressed syllables, my mother's
weeping through the door of her shut room
echoing the metrics of my worried words.
It was the year our family blew apart,
my mother, brothers and sisters and I fleeing
in the push-button Rambler with no reverse
an uncle had taught me to drive. I loved that poem,
finally knew how words the broken and bereft
could alchemize, couldn't wait to get to class,
could hear already in my mind that teacher's
praise. When it came my turn to read, the paper
trembled in my hand, my soft voice cracked,
years passed before I reached the final word,
before she took the glasses from her nose
and cocked her head. *You've skewed your syntax
up* was all she said. I remember nothing else
about her class. That spring her house burned
down, she died inside. *Where haunts the ghost
after the house is gone?* I had several alibis.

FIRST-YEAR TEACHER

During an impassioned lecture
on the three principal parts
of *hang* and *hang*,
I turned from my grainy
etchings across the board
and in the voice
of a would-be pundit
whose moment had finally come,
said, "Please remember, class,
men cannot be hung."

The laughter began
a ripple down the aisle,
a prurient note
passed from desk to desk
until the entire class
let loose a roar.

When they finally gained composure
someone said,
"Couldn't it just be
you've had bad luck
with men?"

Found Poem

Beyond the parking lot of Jack's
Convenience Mart, halfway between
the clinic and Lincoln High, it finds

me, insinuates itself under the sole
of my left shoe, *Winter Poem* by Nikki
Giovanni, scrawled sloppily in ink

and torn from a spiral notebook. I shift
the sack of bread and milk to my right
hand, reach down and pick it up.

Once a snowflake fell
on my brow ... the opening reads,
the script maintaining an artless

integrity that by line three
has already begun to falter...*& I*
loved it   slash   *so much I kissed*

it & it was happy   scribble slash....
Our teenage amanuensis seems to rally
here, writing through without an error

to the end. Following is an assignment
some teacher has made—*Syntax Symbol Diction*—
like a doctor's clipboard checklist, a proper

diagnosis of the poem at hand. No
mention of the heart's terrain, words
that in one breath can break and mend,

render bright the tarnished world
below. How clever that young hand
to let it go.

~~~ AN AMERICAN FAMILY ~~~

St. Peter Said, "That's Good Enough," and He Walked Through

After my father died, he came to me
in a dream, and in a voice, raspy, some
where between a bad Brando and Bogey,
asked if I would accompany him

to the gate, talk him into heaven. It was
cold. March. And night. I didn't
want to go, could think of nothing to advance
his cause, so rose sulking and petulant

and followed him. Saint Peter, flustered, got
out of bed. Name one good thing, he said, waiting.
Finally I recalled the mutilated dog
he once shot to put out of its misery.

We stood there at the weatherless gate, still
strangers, odd pair out of sync until…

THE SABBATICAL

The year my niece grew
ashamed of me, I lived
in a hidden cabin

on my sister's farm—I
who had been the magical
aunt, treasured exotic kin

in the faraway city she could
vanish to for long, lazy weekends
or months at a time in summer,

lunching in grown-up restaurants,
foraging the aisles of bookstores,
museums, and fragile shops

where she alone of all
earth's little girls could touch, beneath
her aunt's protective gaze, anything

she wanted, her fingers soft,
lifting then lighting along the shelves
of antique dolls and porcelain thimbles,

the expensive, loved possessions
of the now long dead. And always
I would catch in my rear-view mirror

the kiss she blew as I pulled out,
having delivered her home again.
How dare I take it all away, come

bumping and rattling into the humdrum
days of her world, lugging behind me
the contents of my own—reduced, even

as she watched, to a single room
where morning until dusk I would languish
in the crumpled gloom of words.

It didn't help she was about to turn
thirteen, her lone ambition painless
initiation into the teenage realm

of cool. It didn't help when the birthday
sleepover girls crept against her
protestations down the weedy path

to witness the strange woman
they'd heard was living there.
I must have seemed

the witch they thought they'd left
behind in the childhood mist
of make-believe: the way, beyond

the window's dim-lit frame, I hovered
at my desk—a cauldron for all they knew,
a doubling bubbling stew of frog

and newt, seasoned thick
with the delicate sweet bones
of their kind. And what of the broken

commode I had dragged from the creek
into my yard and filled with petunias
and ferns, the jars of burgeoning

sprouts along the sill they mistook,
I later learned, for grubs and worms?
Months would pass before she spoke

to me again, before the soft knock
at my cabin door, she on the stoop
asking to borrow the silver hoops

finally in style once more.
She wouldn't come inside or look
at me, as if not looking meant I wasn't

there at all, but back, still, in the distant
gilded land of fairy tale and dream.
When I placed the glittering circles

in her outstretched palm, I saw how her
blonde hair had caught in the maze
some spider had spun over night.

Cool Radio

When she calls and asks
if I will drive her to the mall,
our city's newest labyrinth

of glittering stuff, I know my sister
has come back to me, back
from November's shock of blood,

the exams, the x-rays, the surgeon's
winnowing blade. She is one week
out of the hospital, chemo bag

draped casually across her shoulder,
spilling its slow promise
into her veins. Odd how stylish

in the mall's fluorescent lights,
A Gucci or Von Furstenburg,
its pale blue plastic shiny

as the toy shoes and purses
we used to play grownup in.
I loop my left arm through her

frail right, her tired gate lanky,
almost chic, steady her against
the teenage throng, tattooed

and pierced and spiked, past
racks of skirts and dresses, tier
upon tier of stiletto heels

like the ones our dead mother
in her younger years
suffered so beautifully in.

At the base of the escalator,
beyond The Limited and The Gap,
a girl too young for fashion's

fleeting realm spies the apparatus
around my sister's neck. "Cool
radio," she whispers to no one

as we all step on together.

AN AMERICAN FAMILY

At the grocery store I bought pumpkins,
one for each of us—me, my husband,
and our blond daughter—so I might teach her
the lost art of family, art of mothering

earth, pies a spice cloud from the oven
and the solace of seeds, those tiny
purses of goodness spilling their best kept
secret into our mouths: nothing, nothing

ever lost or wasted. The picture we must
have made there! The little ghost bears
of our breath just out of their summer caves
and the maple loosing its yellow stars

onto our sweaters and hair. I couldn't stop
myself, as we chiseled our lovely symmetry
of mouths and noses and eyes, couldn't stop
imagining a chopper humming over, the surprised

photographer from, say, *Family Life*, leaning
precariously out to freeze the scene forever.
It was then I noticed they weren't carving
at all, the two of them laughing and giggling

as they hammered acorns for eyes into the pulpy
flesh, the grotesque slurs of mouths
a deranged arrangement of brackets and nails
scavenged from the shed, each fat orange

head complete with cornhusk rolled
cigar, a toupee of dead chrysanthemums.
So this was the thanks I got! My Happy Jack
next those creatures my husband

and daughter had dubbed Crack Kills
and Syndrome. A scene more likely
to be caught by some hack from *National
Enquirer*, our story relegated to an inside

page, obscured by the juicier "Man Dies
at Ninety: Pooch Serves as Pall Bearer."
What should I care? If the truth be known,
there were no sweaters and the day

unseasonably warm. My daughter's hair
not blond at all, but the brown bark
of the oak whose stubborn leaves cling
like dirty laundry to its branches,

her father and I living
in sin, bound straight for hell
as his mother continues to warn—
that woman who named me

for the slut I guess, after all, I am.

All Adverbs, Adjectives Too

Odd thing, I thought,
    for a teenager to say she
        despised. The hair-do

of the girl at the table
    next to us I might have
        understood. Or the jock

who yesterday between
    biology class and history
        took back his ring. But why

this sudden announcement
    at the height of our weekly
        outing over burgers and shakes?

I was not her blood,
    but that oddest of creatures,
        soft surrogate body designated

step, the woman loyalty to her
    mother required that she
        hate. How else, in her logic,

to remind me of that? I who
    worshipped at The Church of God
        of Rhetoric, lone walker through

the valley of the shadow of
    words. I watched her face drain
        pale, the laughter fade, fat heart

of a strawberry stopped midair
    between her fingertips and tongue.
        And then that cruel pronouncement,

adamant declaration spewed my way
    in the midst of our frivolity, sending
        me once again to my proper place.

No sooner had she spoken than the light
    returned, the strawberry resuming its
        journey through her penitent lips.

I held a second longer
    the feigned hurt across my face,
        vowed never to let her know

I despise them too.

The Napkin

One night in a pub
on the outskirts of Roanoke,
I sat with my husband

at a table lit only
by the candle's mute flickering
and the small waning moons

of our drinks. I was writing
in my journal, journaling
a journey soon coming

to its end when suddenly,
at the table to our left,
a soft commotion of arms

and hands. I looked
at my husband, lost in some
lost moment of the now

lost day, and then at them,
a subtle, peripheral glance
I had long ago perfected.

I could easily have touched
them—they were that close—lovers,
perhaps, signing to each other

their tongueless words. Each
in turn, their hands rose, bright
wings above the flame's dim

corona, secret negotiations
of finger and thumb.
I was stunned to see

how beautiful he was, as if
in the convoluted logic
of my mind, those devoid

of sound and speech must, too,
be devoid of loveliness.
I could see the silvery sheen

of her nails, glimmer of bracelets
and rings as they mounted the air,
lifting then falling, strafing

the crumbed and waxy
landscape of the table below.
When they left, something

fluttered to the floor, the napkin
they had at intervals been scribbling
on, passing back and forth,

the sweet lexicon of their
hands eluding even them.
My husband reached down,

handed it to me. Slowly
I began to read,
unfolding like lingerie

the delicate layers,
each boneless,
fleshless

syllable
naked before
my eyes: *She*

should be talking
to him, it said, *not writing*
in that book. Poor guy,

he looks so lonely.

~~~ UNMENTIONABLES ~~~

A Suit Our Brother Could Have Worn

In a family loyal to the ghost of our home state,
there's always the renegade

cousin. Old aunt who retreats
at Christmas. The turncoat niece.

Infantries of nephews
threatening to secede. And then to

secede from that. This time it was Mother,
who couldn't believe my sister

and I would darken the door
of that funeral home where

her own dead sister's husband
lay. Not one of them

had shown—not even a card—
when our darling brother

died. The two of us went anyway. Rendezvoused
at a store we knew

on the outskirts of our hometown where
nothing could have prepared

me for what happened there. For the way
my sister turned to me, seized both my

just-washed hands and pressed
them without warning to her burgeoning breasts.

What leap of time and space,
not to mention faith,

had catapulted me to the toilet of the Stop & Save where
I now stood, caressing my younger sister?

She who all her life had prayed for ampleness.
Whose padded bra I'd poke in jest

if she walked past and Mother wasn't looking. Whose
flesh, like jellied mounds, now rose

beneath my startled palms. Later we were shocked
to see our uncle lying there so small, not

half the man he used to be in a suit our
brother could have worn.

Our dry-eyed cousins seemed perplexed when we
began to weep, nieces—not even blood—shaking

in each other's arms above a bible made of papier-mache
and flanked in plastic mums. Finally

someone spoke to comfort us—*You know, he always
could've stood to lose a little weight.*

On our drive back to the Stop & Save, my
sister blew her nose and wiped her eyes

then reached inside her dress and pulled
them out, two small

sacs of silicone she'd ordered on the internet.
These things are killing me, she said,

and rolled her window down. Sometimes I wonder,
still, what passed through the stranger's

mind who found them lying there.

The Living Daylights

She'd beat it out of all
of us, she warned, if we
dared defy her rules,

tried her thinning patience
one more time. Truth is, she
never laid a hand on anyone,

though once, for some small
forgotten truancy, she snatched
me without warning from my play,

swatting at my behind
with a belt she'd grabbed
from its too-convenient hook

on the closet door, and oh
what a sight together there
we made, round and round

the living room, a windmill,
top, fine whirligig, bright wheel
and she the axis to my screeching

spoke. By the time she finally
ceded me the win, not a lick
had grazed the small but quicker

shins that carried me bruise-free
into womanhood, I who fared
no worse than the neighbor kids

who bore into the world deep marks
of defter hands. She's gone
now, benign and hopeless queen

of discipline, the living daylights
beaten, in the end, out of all of us.

UNMENTIONABLES

Odd how my mother's incessant utterings
seemed only an attempt
to unsay the world her eyes,

her ears, her nose, her ever-flitting
hands bore witness to. *Unthinkable,
unspeakable, unheard of,* she would

say, annihilating the bits
and pieces of unpalatable news
that daily came her way.

That unfortunate down the street, she
dubbed the woman who traded
herself for cash to feed

her hungry brood. And the ultimate
obscuring, total obliteration
of the offending word—*unmentionables,*

meaning the clean cotton panties
my sisters and I wore beneath
the pique and organdy

of our dresses and skirts. Sundays
at dinner, it was always
drumstick, dark meat, trotter

she would ask someone to pass,
the word *leg* far too erotic
for her lexicon. Had she not gone

when she did, this is what they would
have done to her: amputate her lower
extremities, or, as the doctor

later, so clearly, put it—cut off
both her legs. How considerate
the gods to have spared her

the indelicacy of those words,
mortification of a different kind.

Death has no manners, Mama—

unspeakable, unthinkable, unutterable—

that unfortunate down the street,
waiting, in the soft, ephemeral
lure of her unmentionables.

SHADOW DANCING

I wish Miss Saylo could've seen
the night my brother said, *Go Limp*,
then swirled me in his arms across

the discotheque, light and lithe,
more graceful than I had ever been,
she who'd put an end to my dancing

days. She was tiny and all pruned up,
like those photos I never understood
of vegetables dressed like people,

ribbed peppers sporting glasses,
tomatoes in tutus and tiaras. She
carried a big stick, nudged to attention

our clavicles and ribs if we slouched
in our pliés or rendered too soft
our arabesques. I tried to do what she

instructed. Pretended to be that leaf
fluttering from its tree, oh, down
and twirling down I went, landing

in a tangled mass amidst the fine
and tutored elegance of the other girls.
When she shouted, *Stop!* it took a moment

to realize she was talking to me,
though grace of some sudden other
kind made her wait until later

to relegate me to the stool
by the record player
where until semester's end

I would raise and lower the needle
at her command. So it was she
I thought of years later,

in the unschooled pedagogy
of my brother's arms, beautiful
in his white suit, the pink shirt

with pearl buttons he would keep
for years, long after the disease
had ravaged him, the Bus Stop

and the Hustle having entered, too,
oblivion's faithful realm. *Go
limp*, was all he said, and I did,

each lift and trill of the Bee Gees'
bright falsettos waking the long
muted language of my body.

Even Andy was not dead yet.

My Brother's Star

I'm healed, my brother said,
his voice trembling, small quakes
of joy through the wires

connecting the ghostly morning
of his far coast with the early afternoon
of mine. It was late August. I wanted

so badly to believe, I let myself.
I who'd begun to pray for miracles,
the urgency of my pleas

rising exponentially with the slow
sloughing off of his white cells.
When I saw him in September,

he seemed even more diminished,
though he said it again—*I'm healed.*
Again and again he said it, at

the oddest times. To the cashier
in the florist shop when he ordered
roses for the doctors he would no

longer need. Once I heard him
whisper it to the juniper in his back
yard. The leaves, I swear, began to flutter

though there was no breeze. As I
was packing to fly home again, he led
me to his closet, took from its wire

hanger his most beautiful shirt
and handed it to me, the sweet smell
of his dwindling body draped now across

my arms. In October his St. Christopher
traveled back with Allen. With Rosie,
his favorite robe. But when Trisha

came home with his star, spikes
of golden sheen haloed in silvery
dust, cherished ornament he placed

each year atop his Christmas tree, I
began to scream. Into the startled face
of the sister I adored. November.

He had given her his star.

And I knew, finally, what
my brother meant. What he meant
when he said, *I'm healed.*

And began giving his things away.

QUESTIONS FOR PLUTO

QUESTIONS FOR PLUTO

Did the authorities
knock, too,
at your door,
the sun
you had always
counted on
not yet
fully risen
to his high place?

And who was that man,
hard, cold star
pinned
to the midnight blue
of his chest,
telling,
yes, telling you
you were not,
after all,
who you thought
you were.

Last Day

for Kate Berryman

Readying for the morning errands, you bundled
baby Sarah, Martha off already
to her daily dose of history, language arts.
*You won't have to worry about me
anymore,* he said, donning a coat and scarf.
You'd heard it all before, who'd born him to exhaustion, loved him well.

I, too, shopped that morning, met my husband
later at KFC—2 wing deals, 2 sweet teas—
where beyond the rippling window that sudden first white.
It's snowing! I gasped. *Spitting,* he corrected, as like
a school girl lured from the day's unfinished lessons,
I pressed my nose to the glass.

That night, wine and the gas logs blazing, Keillor on the radio
reading your husband's poem. How had he done it, my
husband wanted to know when I mentioned the suicide.
And in my happy ignorance so
began the stunning last revision
of his plan.

THE NOTES

for Nick Flynn

You dreamt your mother's
scrawled in pencil on a brown paper bag,
and in the bag, huddled at the bottom, six baby mice.
Ah, but the care my husband took!
Classic font laid meticulously down
against the finest bond,
brandished,
even,
with epigraphs.
Twice that week he'd interrupted the morning's work
to solicit my better memory—a couplet
of rich prosody, resonant line of prose. Words,
throughout the single decade of our love,
the two of us had cherished, I unwitting
collaborator of his final masterpiece.
You dreamt the bag
smoldering
from the top down
as your mother's voice
released into the night.
Dreamt the mice growing wilder
as it burned,
their only way out,
if ever,
through the fire.

How It Is in Their Clothes

for Maxine Kumin

A month after your friend's death
you put on her blue blazer, dipped
your hand into the left pocket
to find only a hole, in the right
a parking ticket
plucked from the windshield
of her old sedan, truant car
that would idle later
at the scene
of her final
crime.

Three seasons before I could touch
my husband's clothes, take them down
from their racks, slip my body
into the arms of the handsome
tweed I had loved him in.
I, too, foraged each pocket.
In the right, a single fortune
cookie, hermetically

sealed still in cellophane.
In his left,
as in hers,
a hole.

To Nicholas and Frieda Hughes

O, little birds, what was it like
falling, that night,
to sleep, your beds
the warm, safe nests

she had made for you, her face that would
finally fade
like details of
the fairy tale

she had weaned you on. And how did
it feel, unfeath-
ered, still, that long-
est other fall-

ing?

SOLACE

Each morning in my mailbox
or tucked into a quiet cove
of my front porch, another
burden of solace
reminding me again
my husband is dead.

Last week, an oval cardboard box
decoupaged in stars, inside, its nested
offering—a cache of still-warm eggs
gleaned from my neighbor's henhouse.

Yesterday, a Peruvian prayer shawl,
the warp and weft of its holy weave
climbing, like girders of a bridge,
its sturdy warmth.

And today this handmade flute,
turned and hollowed and carved
by Laughing Crow, enigmatic
shaman of some distant plain.

See its little row of holes
lined up like perfect planets,
as if having not yet learned
the universe had collapsed.

See my lips pressed to the tiny
breathless gape of its own mouth.
As if my lungs could conjure anything.
As if it were the one needing to be saved.

Whistle-Speak

Three weeks after your death
I found them, dog-eared,
flagged and marked, colorful
brochures you hoped

to tempt me with, a trip
you'd planned for years
to that tiny drift of islands
courting Africa's golden

cheek. Remnants of old
volcanoes, fallen ash
and chard, each island
a realm of gorges and ravines

radiating from their centers
like spokes of a wheel. Who
wouldn't want to go there,
where the second native language

is that of birds, shepherds whistling
their messages to an ear cocked miles
away? Where even insults mimic
the mating songs of doves. See

how this old denizen folds his little
finger, presses tight against his tongue
and blows, free hand a makeshift
megaphone cupping conjured sound,

a trill, a chirp, a squawk
surfing the crags and slopes
of no man's land. *It can be used
for anything*, the caption reads:

Call to your friend.
Gather home your children.
Find, in a crowd, the husband
you've somehow lost.

Pear Moonshine

for Sue Campbell and Candy Butler

One night, the darkest winter of my life,
my husband not three cycles dead, I
opened the kitchen door to a quiet knock

and there in the starless gloom
of my back porch, two women bearing
gifts. In Candy's outstretched hands

a pot of homemade soup, in Sue's,
a jar of swollen pears embalmed
in liquid fire. When I reached

to fetch three tumblers down, the two began
to laugh, removed the offending vessels
from my startled hands and returned

them to their rightful place again. Sue
led me to the living room by the hearth
as Candy spun the gold corona

of its lid, drank deep and passed
the jar to Sue then on to me, the ghostly
triad of our lips leaving their own

soft crescents along the rim. Outside
no star had yet to show, no other
moon to light the snow that all day

long had kept me weeping close
to the sputtering flames. We drank
and passed the waning jar and drank

again until the glacier of my pain
began to break, a thousand icy floes
drifting down the river of my grief

and then we ate the soup.

Cathy Smith Bowers, North Carolina Poet Laureate 2010–2012, was born and grew up in Lancaster, South Carolina. She was educated at University of South Carolina-Lancaster, Winthrop University, the University of Oxford, and the Haden Institute. Her poems have appeared widely in publications such as *The Atlantic Monthly*, *The Georgia Review*, *Poetry*, *The Southern Review*, *The Kenyon Review*, and *Ploughshares*, and have been featured on *The Writer's Almanac with Garrison Keillor* and *Poetry Daily*. She is a winner of The General Electric Award, recipient of a South Carolina Poetry Fellowship, and winner of The South Carolina Arts Commission Fiction Project. She served for many years as poet-in-residence at Queens University of Charlotte where she received the 2002 JB Fuqua Distinguished Educator Award, and now teaches in the Queens low-residency MFA program and at Wofford College. Her first book, *The Love That Ended Yesterday in Texas*, was the inaugural winner of The Texas Tech University Press First Book Competition. She lives in the North Carolina foothills of the Blue Ridge Mountains.

About the Cover Artist

Cover artist **CHUCK DAVIS** lives in Liberty, Missouri, and makes his living as an artist, working primarily with oils. His paintings can be found in galleries and private collections around the world. To see more of his paintings, visit his Facebook page at www.facebook.com/ChuckDavisArtistPage.